Dagger of the Mind

Solving the Mystery of Shakespeare's Death

ALSO BY J. E. WALSH

NONFICTION

Emily Dickinson In Love: the Case for Otis Lord

When the Laughing Stopped: The Strange, Sad Death of Will Rogers

The Night Casey Was Born: The True Story of a Great American Ballad, "Casey at the Bat"

Walking Shadows: Orson Welles, William Randolph Hearst, and "Citizen Kane"

The Execution of Major Andre

Moonlight: Abraham Lincoln and the Almanac Trial

Darkling I Listen: The Last Days and Death of John Keats

Midnight Dreary: The Mysterious Death of Edgar Allen Poe

Unraveling Piltdown: The Science Fraud of the Century and Its Solution

The Shadows Rise: Abraham Lincoln and the Anne Rutledge Legend

This Brief Tragedy: Unraveling the Todd-Dickinson Affair

Into My Own: The English Years of Robert Frost

The Bones of St. Peter: A Full Account of the Search for the Apostle's Body

Plumes in the Dust: The Love Affair of Edgar Allan Poe and Fanny Osgood

Night on Fire: The First Complete Account of John Paul Jones's Greatest Battle

One Day at Kitty Hawk: The Untold Story of the Wright Brothers and the Airplane

The Hidden Life of Emily Dickinson

Poe the Detective: The Curious Circumstances behind the Mystery of Marie Roget

Strange Harp, Strange Symphony: The Life of Francis Thompson

The Letters of Francis Thompson (Collected, Annotated)

The Shroud: The Story of the Holy Shroud of Turin

FICTION

The Man Who Buried Jesus: A Mystery Novel

In Loving Memory of
Matthew Owen Walsh
1961–2013
One of Life's true originals

ARIZONA CENTER FOR
MEDIEVAL & RENAISSANCE STUDIES
OCCASIONAL PUBLICATIONS

VOLUME 6

DAGGER OF THE MIND

SOLVING THE MYSTERY OF SHAKESPEARE'S DEATH

JOHN EVANGELIST WALSH

ARIZONA CENTER FOR MEDIEVAL

ACMRS

AND RENAISSANCE STUDIES

Tempe, Arizona
2013

THE ARIZONA CENTER FOR

MEDIEVAL &
RENAISSANCE
STUDIES

Published by ACMRS (Arizona Center for Medieval and Renaissance Studies)
Tempe, Arizona

Library of Congress Cataloging-in-Publication Data

Walsh, John Evangelist, 1927- author.
  Dagger of the Mind : Solving The Mystery of Shakespeare's Death / John E. Walsh.
       pages cm. -- (ACMRS Occasional Publications ; Volume 6)
  Includes bibliographical references and index.
  ISBN 978-0-86698-500-0 (alk. paper)
1. Shakespeare, William, 1564-1616--Death and burial. 2. Dramatists, English-
-Early modern, 1500-1700--Biography. 3. Stratford-upon-Avon (England)--
Biography. I. Title.
  PR2908.W35 2013
  822.3'3--dc23
                                                                        2013041850

∞
This book is made to last.
It is set in Adobe Kepler Std
and printed on acid-free paper to library specifications.
Printed in the United States of America

Contents

ACKNOWLEDGMENTS

My debt is a large one to all those dedicated scholars and investigators who did their work and did it so well during more than three centuries. Uncovering much vital information about the poet personally, they also provided stimulating discussion of their discoveries. Their names, what they contributed to my own treatment of the subject, and my warm gratitude may be read in the detailed analyses offered in the notes.

To Professor Thomas P. Roche, Jr., Princeton University *emeritus*, and Professor Richard Knowles, University of Wisconsin *emeritus*, go my sincere thanks for their informed and sympathetic readings of the book in manuscript, and their helpful comments.

Most particularly I thank my son Timothy A. Walsh for his careful and knowing review of these chapters as they developed.

J. E. Walsh

ILLUSTRATIONS

Fig. 1: Under this plain granite slab in the chancel of Holy Trinity Church in Stratford rest Shakespeare's remains. See p. 77 for the inscription.

PROLOGUE:
STRANGE BUSINESS

This is as strange a maze as ere men trod,
And there is in this business more than
Nature was ever conduct of....
The Tempest

"But there is *no* mystery about Shakespeare's death. It was quite a normal one. Otherwise we'd certainly have long since heard about it."

Several times during my studies for this book those or similar words were directed at me, not always calmly, by persons whose scholarship gave them the right to speak on the question. Each time in sober reply I ventured to ask why, if such was the case, a total blank surrounds that lamented event — when and where he died, how he died, of what specific cause, suddenly or after a lengthy illness, at home or elsewhere, attended or alone, what time of day or night. Of all these things no one today can give the least account (the sole stray attempt, occurring long afterward, will be addressed in a moment).

"Mere quirks of history," I was told with finality, "accidental oversights well understood by historians of that distant time." Incredulous, I couldn't help asking, "And you are quite *satisfied* with that?"

A mystery in the classic modern sense the poet's death may not be, with one neatly portrayed crime to be unraveled, a single perpetrator to be caught. Yet a veritable mystery it is, crying out for solution. Who that has an interest in the world's greatest writer does not wish to know how and why death came for him while he was yet, though retired, in the fullness of his powers? In tracking a myriad of facts, following a trail long grown cold, more than once I have felt I was uncovering things never meant to be remembered, never meant to be known to anyone outside the Shakespeare family.

Despite what scholars generally assume as to the paucity of information surviving from that remote era, the silence hovering over *this* death is more than passing strange. Many members of his large family, for instance, outlived him by many years (wife, two daughters and their husbands, a granddaughter, two grandsons, a sister, three nephews, and assorted in-laws on his wife's side), yet none provided any slightest bit of information as to the circumstances of his death. Nor did any word come from his Stratford friends or his London theater colleagues. Only a single brief mention exists claiming to give some casual word of his last moments, but it is an unsupported, out-of-the-way diary entry made many years after the fact (1663, by the newly arrived Vicar of Holy Trinity church in Stratford where the poet lies buried). Giving no source, the brief entry claims that Shakespeare succumbed to a "feavour" supposedly contracted after a night of drinking at a "merrie meeting" with friends, a claim for which no least documentation exists. Also, as has often been pointed out, such an end hardly fits the retired actor-playwright who was never known for convivial habits. A respectable family man, in his retirement he enjoyed wealth, personal prestige, and high social rank, occupied the town's best house, and owned much land in the area. His overriding ambition during these latter years was to raise, through his two daughters, his family to lasting social prominence.[1]

Only since about 1850 has the topic of Shakespeare's death received serious biographical attention, with a few writers offering brief, unsupported theories — all lacking both hard evidence and convincing detail. Several diseases have been proposed including Bright's and typhoid. Also on the list are a stroke, pneumonia, a brain hemorrhage, and the unidentified "feavour," but, again, devoid of anything like hard evidence. Inevitably, even murder and suicide have been suggested, but on grounds barely above whimsy.

By now it may appear a futile endeavor to make the attempt at a solution yet again, but that of course is precisely why one more attempt is warranted — drawing on the accumulated study and research of so many dedicated Shakespeare scholars over the decades. In their work, in fact, as I read the record after long and careful perusal, the necessary clues *are* available, lying unrecognized in a random assortment of old books and articles, and, most particularly, in original documents from his own time. Three of these documents, in fact, prove to be at the heart of the case, not only internally as texts but externally for what they point to and uncover about the progress of daily affairs in Stratford.

1) Shakespeare's last will and testament, here revealed as one of literature's most fascinating artifacts, the unexpected source of much vital information when put under close analysis.

2) A private agreement he signed — in secret, as it appears — in the vexed matter of Stratford's bitter "enclosure" battle (concerning the use of land) between ordinary Stratfordians and the town's moneyed interests.

---

1 To anticipate: very probably a "merrie meeting" of some kind did take place. But it was to celebrate the wedding of his daughter Judith, and occurred two and a half months before his death. The incident is treated in its proper place below.

3) The minutes of a session of Stratford's stern Ecclesiastical Court, known to all as the "Bawdy Court" because it dealt so largely with sexual matters. In this respect the concern is not with Shakespeare but with his scapegrace son-in-law.

My opening chapter lays out in narrative sequence the events of the poet's final year, setting the scene to the fullest extent permitted by the evidence, and with only a bare minimum of commentary. Then in Chapters Two, Three, and Four each of those foreshadowed events is more fully developed, its true significance made plain. In Chapters Five and Six, calling on every available fact — more numerous than most people would guess — while drawing out hidden, submerged, and "latent" meanings, I offer the promised solution. In those same two chapters, as reasonable (I trust) climaxes to my lengthy analysis of the three documents above listed, I offer three brief wrap-up scenes in the form of reconstructed narratives. Their objective reality, strongly indicated, rests on my own conclusions from the evidence previously laid out. While not usual in a scholarly work, they have value, I feel, in strengthening and clarifying the facts and interpretation naturally occurring in the flow of the ongoing argument. They are of course fully identified as conjecture.

The first such scene pictures a serious clash between old friend Thomas Greene and the irate poet at New Place, the Shakespeare home. It is the pivotal, precipitating encounter leading to the end. The second such scene describes a happy visit to the ailing Shakespeare by his friend and neighbor Hamnet Sadler. The third scene shows Shakespeare's solicitor Francis Collins, then engaged in drawing up the bedridden poet's will, bringing to him at New Place the culminating revelation that seals his fate. Of course these special scenes have been entirely derived and written under strict control of what is actually known as undoubted fact, and what may legitimately be held probable.

Chapter Seven adds a final point of interest, one that I believe proves to be of peculiar significance.

In the Stratford parish church, Holy Trinity, on April 25, 1616 — two days after his death — before the main altar and just inside the chancel railing to the left of center, a grave was dug and into it Shakespeare's coffin was lowered. Watching the solemn ceremony from the crowded pews would have been some dozen members of his family including his wife Anne and the two daughters with their husbands, along with a crowd of relatives and friends and no doubt a contingent of curious townsfolk. Somewhat later over the grave was fitted a broad, flat slab of granite, level with the surrounding floor. Cut into the slab's stippled gray surface was a four-line verse warning that the body underneath must never be disturbed: "Cursed be he that moves my bones," threatens the concluding line. It was some 350 years after the burial that I first stood in that same church at the altar rail gazing down at the inscribed granite slab. As I stared, picturing the poet as he had looked, walked, and talked in life, I felt the first sharp stab of curiosity as to what cause, precisely, had brought him there when only fifty-three years of age, not young, but not old, either, not even for that time.

Now I am satisfied that I know, and it is not a pleasant or a pretty tale. In Shakespeare's own hands I think it might have become a story to rival any of his great tragedies. Further, as it turns out, behind the last fatal moment there *was* one precipitating event to be unraveled, and a single perpetrator to be caught, if we may call him that.

ABOUT THIS BOOK'S TITLE

The phrase, of course, is Macbeth's, whose employment of it is quite different from mine. For him the dagger he sees in the air, "the handle toward my hand," does not exist. It is a hallucination, a *projection* of his mind, which is not my meaning at all. But the phrase is an evocative and finely flexible one, in a different sense exactly capturing my solution to the mystery, so I could not pass it up. That claim, I trust, will justify itself well before the last page is turned.

SOLVING THE MYSTERY OF SHAKESPEARE'S DEATH

Give order that these bodies
High on a stage be placed to the view,
And let me speak to the yet unknowing world
How these things came about . . .

Hamlet

1.
MR SHAKESPEARE & FAMILY

In the big, five-gabled house on Chapel Street in Stratford-upon-Avon everything was in proper order. Parlors, dining room, bedrooms, the master's study, all had been given a final appraising look. For an entire month the master of the house had been away on business in London, his lengthiest absence from home in years. Today he was due back and at any moment his carriage would swing round the corner from Chapel Lane to come clattering up the street. Master Shakespeare, it was known, liked a well-run, well-set-up house, and his wife during their thirty-two years of marriage always made sure he had it.

They'd owned the big house, called New Place, for almost twenty of those thirty-two years, buying it with the first substantial proceeds of his playwriting, especially the smash-hit *Romeo and Juliet,* his first big success.[1] At first when he left home he'd do his writing in his London lodgings where he had the stimulus of proximity to fellow writers, actors, and the stage itself, first at The Theatre, London's first playhouse, then the Rose, the Swan, and finally The Globe. Later, disliking the long separation from his family, he'd come home to write for weeks or a month, finding ease and inspiration in Stratford's saner, serener atmosphere. A pretty little town on the banks of the gently-flowing Avon, it was some hundred miles north of the capital.

That afternoon as expected Shakespeare's carriage came rolling up to the gate in the high brick wall that enclosed the broad front lawn. In the house he was greeted by his wife Anne and his younger daughter, Judith, both wishing him a happy fifty-second birthday. A contented man, sound in mind and body, after almost thirty grueling years in the theater as writer and actor, William Shakespeare was living the life of semi-retirement he'd long planned. Now a man of wealth and property, he had a good, steady income derived from his shares in his old acting company, and his extensive local investments. No one had the least cause to suspect that it would all end so soon.

---

1 "Smash-hit" sounds like an anachronism. But the Elizabethan theater had its boffo events, too, not unlike Broadway today except that there were no "long runs" then. But that *Romeo and Juliet* was Shakespeare's breakthrough offering after two or three minor successes is quite clear from the record.

The date of his return from his lengthy London stay was Thursday, April 23, 1615, the very day he'd welcomed the start of his fifty-second year. As he accepted the loving wishes of his wife and daughter, the master of New Place had exactly a year to the day to live.

It would speed by fairly quickly, that final year, not always pleasantly, but mostly in the quiet enjoyment of family matters and the occasional mild stimulus of town affairs. Only three blocks over, in the house on Henley Street where he'd been born, lived his sister Joan with her husband and three boys, the oldest now nearly sixteen. Two blocks in the opposite direction, in a picturesque old house on Old Town Road, lived his eldest daughter, Susanna. Married to a doctor, one of the most prominent in the county, John Hall, after eight years Susanna had produced only one child, a girl, Elizabeth, now seven. Still at home in New Place and unmarried at age thirty was his daughter Judith. If she'd been less choosy, with a father who was one of the day's most famous and affluent authors, she could have been married many times over. Lately she'd begun to show an interest in one young man, Thomas Quiney, but as often happens, the young man didn't at all suit her father's wishes for a son-in-law. To make matters worse, Quiney was younger by four years than Judith, and was the son of one of Shakespeare's oldest friends.

Still, it wasn't really the same in Stratford any more, not as it was when he first went away. Six of the people who meant most to him were dead — his father and mother, all three of his brothers, Edmund, Richard, and Gilbert, and his own eleven-year-old son, Hamnet. The first of the three brothers to die, Edmund, had followed him to London to become an actor, and aided by his brother's influence he'd begun to catch on fairly well. But at only twenty-six he was dead, buried in a London churchyard. Gilbert, who stayed in Stratford, had lived into his forties, dying in 1612, but Richard, who died the next year, had been only thirty-eight.

The loss of his son Hamnet, who'd been Judith's twin, in the summer of 1596, had dealt him his severest blow to date, his profound grief finding an outlet in a play he was then writing, *The Life and Death of King John*. In it a character accused of too much grieving over the death of a loved one responds with quietly searing words that achingly express the awful sorrow of losing a child:

> Grief fills the room up of my absent child,
> Lies in his bed, walks up and down with me,
> Puts on his pretty looks, repeats his words,
> Remembers me of all his gracious parts,
> Stuffs out his vacant garments with his form
> Then have I reason to be fond of grief. . . .

Underneath the grief, greatly intensifying it, was his acute disappointment at losing his sole male heir. His personal dream of the future had included a prosperous, prominent line of descendants built on the large estate he hoped to accumulate

and leave behind. He and Anne might have had more children, but for some unknown reason they didn't (some physical change in Anne after the birth of her
twins had perhaps blocked further conceptions). As the years went on his two
girls became his hope, and in 1615, though Susanna was then thirty-two and Judith barely two years younger, both somewhat advanced for childbearing, he still
looked eagerly for grandsons.

Old neighbors and childhood friends were also on hand to make life in Stratford more congenial, some living no further off than a block or two. Round on
Sheep Street were the Sadlers (the Shakespeare twins had been named for them),
and the Tylers. A bit further away, in High Street, were the Rogers, the Smiths, and
the Quineys (with their son Thomas plotting uneasily how to draw a kind look
and a good word from Judith's father, a man he'd known all his life. Judith, too,
he'd always known, but only recently had he begun to see her as a desirable, full-
grown woman).

In Chapel Street itself resided, in substantial houses of their own, three families that had long been a part of the Shakespeares' daily lives, the Courts, the
Reynolds, and the Shaws. At the other end of town, a less populated area near
the College and Holy Trinity Church, were another family of Reynolds, and the
Greenes, distant cousins of the Shakespeares.

Besides the high station gained for him among his townsmen by his reputation as poet and playwright, he'd also managed to enter the ranks of the gen-
try, much above the level of his birth. In 1596, as soon as he'd gathered sufficient
funds, in his father's name he applied for a family coat of arms. Eventually one was
granted, and from that time he enjoyed the right to be known as, and to sign himself, *gentleman*. In the social strata of town and county he was near the top.

Only once did his determined drive to genteel status for his family receive a
setback, a particularly ugly incident that took place soon after his retreat to Stratford. To say the least it was a strange affair, and even now, after so much study of the
facts by so many critics, it is not easy to say just what happened, or what may have
been its impact in the community. To make matters worse it involved his admired
daughter Susanna, at age thirty a wife and mother, noted for her high intelligence,
strict morality, and, as her own family testified, a rarely understanding heart.

In the summer of 1613 a rumor ran through Stratford society that Susanna Hall
had been caught in an act of adultery with a local man. Names and places were
specified, all relating to Stratford, all well-known. The famous playwright's daughter, said the whispers, had recently and perhaps more than once shared a bed with a
certain Ralph Smith, proprietor of a haberdashery shop. The place of the tryst, supposedly, was the home of one John Palmer, otherwise of no known significance.

How Shakespeare and his son-in-law, John Hall, Susanna's husband, picked
up the gossip is not known. In any case they had no sooner heard the shocking tale
than they took action, somehow managing to uncover the source of the rumor.

Surprisingly, it turned out to be a young man, John Lane, twenty-three years of age, the son of a prominent Stratford family well known to the Shakespeares. Lane's sister, in fact, was married to a cousin of Shakespeare, John Greene (whose brother Thomas, the town clerk, will make his own appearance further along in these pages). The supposed seducer, Ralph (or Rafe) Smith, aged thirty-five and married, was also linked to the Shakespeare circle. His father, a vintner and town alderman, was a relative of Hamnet Sadler, one of Shakespeare's oldest friends.

Acting quickly, Shakespeare and Hall brought suit against Lane for defamation, which for some reason was filed not at Stratford but in the Bishop's Court in Worcester. The case was called on July 15, 1613, no doubt with Shakespeare, Hall, Judith, Joan Hart, and perhaps a few of Susanna's own family sitting in the audience. The accused woman herself may have been on hand, bravely facing the distasteful ordeal.

Lane, however, disobeying the court summons, failed to show up, an absence which didn't interrupt the proceedings. At least one witness was heard, Robert Whattcott (or Whatcote) of Stratford, and he firmly fixed on Lane full responsibility for the slander (apparently also in some way refuting it). "About five weeks past," swore Whattcott, "the defendant reported that the plaintiff had the runninge of the raynes & had been caught with Rafe Smith at John Palmer's." (A Stratford resident of no known connection with Shakespeare, Whatcott later became a signatory to his will. He may at the time have been a "friend" of the poet's, or perhaps one of his servants, as some biographers have it. His curious phrase "runninge of the raynes" adds its own unexpected complication to the story, to be noticed presently).

The surviving record is bare of any witnesses who may have spoken in support of Lane, or against Susanna, and in fact there may have been none of either. The bishop, hearing no additional adverse testimony against her, found for Susanna. John Lane he excommunicated, a drastic action which may show that private information was available to him.

Shakespeare biographers tend to dismiss the Lane accusation against the poet's daughter as beneath notice, according it little or no discussion. The fact of the charge and the outcome of the Worcester trial are reported, but none asks the obvious question: why, granting Susanna's innocence, would Lane have done such a thing, daring to attack one of the town's leading families, naming names? On one later occasion, as is always pointed out, Lane was convicted of public drunkenness, and was embroiled in one or two of the town's more contentious issues. Yet he was otherwise a respected member of the community, known to many of the same people who knew and were friendly with the Halls and Shakespeare.

The good people of Stratford, keenly responsive to scandal in their midst, aware that Susanna had won her case only by default, certainly did not allow the juicy tale of infidelity to pass in silence. The rampant gossip touching his loved and much admired daughter, whom he saw as inheritor to some extent of his

Fig. 2: William Shakespeare about as he looked at his death. Bust from the wall monument above his grave in Holy Trinity Church, Stratford. Disliked by some Shakespeareans as not sufficiently intellectual looking, the bust was certainly approved by Mrs. Shakespeare and other family members.

talent, must have pained the poet intensely. "Witty above her sex," declares Susanna's gravestone in Holy Trinity Church (she died in 1649), also noting, as if it were a family tradition, "Something of Shakespeare was in that." The epitaph also notes her upright moral character ("Wise to salvation was good Mistress Hall"), as well as her ready compassion for the pain of others:

> . . . hast ne'er a teare
> To weep with her that wept with all?
> That wept, yet set herself to cheere
> Them up with comforts cordiall.
> Her love shall live, her mercy spread,
> When thou has ne'er a teare to shed.

Further upsetting the quiet progress of that final year were irritating situations that had begun some time previously and were only then coming to a head. One, apparently minor, was a lawsuit Shakespeare filed while in London to recover certain documents connected with his latest property purchase. Buying a house near the Thames in London's Blackfriars district, he was surprised to find that many of the related documents — "letters patent, deedes, Charters, escripts, evidences,

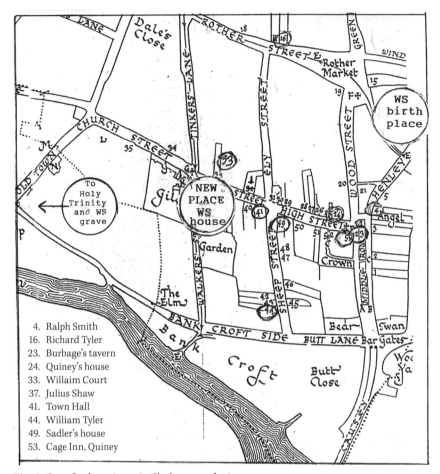

Fig. 3: Stratford-on-Avon in Shakespeare's time.

muniments, and all writeings whatsoever," as the suit specified — were being strangely withheld by the owners. Suing them in a London court, he was back in Stratford more than a month before word came that he'd won his case. Known as the Gate-House, the Blackfriars residence was probably intended for his own and his family's use while in London, but no sooner was it purchased than it was rented to one John Robinson, a name unconnected to Shakespeare otherwise. In curious fashion it will surface again near the end of that final year.

Far more troublesome than the Blackfriars property was an embroilment that for some two years had stirred up and seriously divided all of Stratford. This concerned the attempt — sudden, almost surreptitious — by a few wealthier residents to enclose the common lands. The act of "enclosure," as it was called, had become a burning issue across England, exciting the strongest feelings in one anxious community after another. Certain landowners wanted to change the old medieval system of renting small growing patches to local farmers to one which combined them into larger fields for cattle and sheep grazing, a far more lucrative use. Often, by reducing the amount of arable acreage accessible to ordinary people, the move worked a drastic change. In not a few towns where enclosure had succeeded a large part of the population had either been reduced to poverty or had sold up and moved out. Those who remained could only stand and watch as their town sank into slow decay. Mob action and riots were not unknown where the spectre of enclosure was raised.

Shakespeare, owner of several hundred acres in the affected area just north of Stratford, was not among those landowners who were moving for enclosure. But neither did he oppose them, not even when asked. The hard-pressed town Council, girding for a court fight to halt the move, had specifically requested his help, asking that he lend his name and reputation to the fight on behalf of the town's working men. Quietly he refused and then went further. If enclosure took place, he saw, then the value of his own lands might be considerably diminished, and to counter this threat he acted swiftly and decisively. From the prospective enclosers he obtained a promise in writing that any loss he might suffer would be reimbursed. It was a private guarantee, and at the time the instrument was not made public. Only at the close of his final year, when he had a number of other matters to agitate and trouble him, would word of his secret agreement with the enclosers leak out, bringing him great embarrassment and sore distress.

As a recent biographer has said, the enclosure episode "reveals a hitherto unseen side to the playwright of the people; while publically supporting their aims, and no doubt genuinely sympathizing in private, he was quietly hedging his bets by doing clandestine deals with the enemy". He would take no chance on losing the fortune, or any part of it, on which he hoped to found a family dynasty. That was the grand design and hope of his life (made crystal clear, as shortly will be seen, in his will).

What Shakespeare feared most during that final year happened. In the fall of 1615 the young scamp (as Shakespeare thought of him) Thomas Quiney proposed to Judith and was accepted. The proprietor of a small tavern in Bridge Street, the twenty-seven-year-old Quiney had something of a reputation as a drinker, as well as a ladies' man. Intelligent, handsome, a charmer, he was well-educated and, unlike many then, wrote a good hand. But he lacked ambition, and tended to be irresponsible, which made his being four years younger than Judith even less palatable to his prospective father-in-law.

On top of that, everyone in town knew that Mistress Shakespeare would bring with her a handsome marriage-portion, some hundred pounds at least (in a day when working men raised families comfortably on a pound a month). When word got around that young Quiney had won the prize, heads nodded, knowingly.

At first the disgusted Shakespeare held out against his daughter's choice. In the end he gave in, though not without setting some conditions. Quiney must match Judith's marriage-portion, he specified — it would be 150 pounds — by settling on the bride a similar amount in land or stock. No doubt a bit staggered by the condition, Quiney may have complained about the size of the obligation, a huge one for a young man, even a young man whose family was well fixed. Asking for time to comply, he at last agreed, and with that the grudgingly satisfied Shakespeare proceeded to alter his will. The bulk of his estate would still go to his elder daughter Susanna and her thoroughly reliable husband, Dr. Hall. But to Tom and Judy would go an additional three hundred pounds, enough to make sure that the Shakespeare grandchildren grew up in more than easy circumstances.

Quiney's next move was reassuring. On his own he arranged to take over another, much larger tavern in Stratford with a perfect location quite at the town's business center, the popular Cage Inn standing at the corner of High and Wood Streets. With this decisive sign of growing maturity in his son-in-law-elect, the doubtful Shakespeare could only have been pleased. Lurking unsuspected in the background, however, was a much less pleasant fact, one destined to play a crucial part in the events of that final, fatal year.

One night in the summer of 1615, several months before he made his formal proposal of marriage to Judith, the self-indulgent young Master Quiney had taken to bed with him another young woman of Stratford, a single girl named Margaret Wheeler. On the day that he asked the poet's daughter to be his wife, the unlucky Margaret was some four months pregnant.

Fig. 4: In this large house in Stratford Shakespeare was born and raised. Here he brought his wife Anne and here his three children were born (and one died). He was aged 23 or so when he left it to try his hand on the London stage. For long it remained in the family, passing to his sister Joan, then to her children, and later a grand-nephew. At the door stands the author.

2.
THE SILVER GILT BOWL

In the third week of January 1616, Francis Collins, the Shakespeares' solicitor and an old acquaintance, walked up to the front door of New Place and jangled the bell-pull. He'd been sent for by Shakespeare, who explained that he wanted to make a few changes in his will, first executed some years before. Inside the house as the two sat reading over the old will, Collins listened carefully and made precise notes. The changes he wanted, explained the poet, were meant to take account of his daughter's upcoming wedding and her altered status, changes which would have some effect on those parts of the will relating to the already married Susanna, and perhaps to Mrs. Shakespeare.

Some days later Collins, consulting his notes of the session with his client at New Place, proceeded with his own hand to draw up the revised instrument. Of moderate length compared to the wills of some of Collins' other wealthy clients, it covered two and a half sheets of foolscap (good rag paper, each sheet measuring about twelve by fifteen inches, the standard), one side only. The style of script was the usual one then for legal papers, what was called the secretary hand, full of small flourishes and exaggerated strokes (changing, even as Collins wrote, to the simpler Italian hand, today's comfortably readable form).

It still exists, the fascinating original document that solicitor Collins penned that January day in Stratford, and in surprisingly good physical condition. Now carefully preserved under glass in a special case, it is one of the prized possessions of London's Public Record Office. But it is not now as Collins first drew it up. Shortly after its completion a number of alterations were made in it — deletions by a stroke of the pen and scribbled interlineations — which make it, properly analyzed, a prime piece of evidence in the investigation of the poet's death.

That the will as it stands was made in two stages — an original later altered — is a fact long understood and easily grasped from the evidence of the will itself. There are several changes, the major one being *a complete rewrite of the original page one*. The fact of the rewrite is not stated, but under close analysis is readily demonstrated.

On the second of the three sheets, at the very top, occur two lines of writing. They are followed by three lines that have been deleted (struck out by long strokes of the pen). The three deleted lines do not follow the sense of the two lines that precede them, but the two upper lines are linked with the bottom of the existing page one. Only a minute's study of the two pages is sufficient to show that the original first sheet has been discarded, and the present one substituted. (See the facsimile, pp. 18–20.)

The three *deleted* lines on the top of the present page two, it is obvious, continued whatever was originally written on the bottom of the discarded page one. That the two *undeleted* lines above them were run-overs, crowded along the vacant top margin of page two, also is obvious. In fact, on the bottom of page one the last dozen lines have been severely squeezed together, deliberately cramped, in the hope of fitting all the new matter on that revised first page. Still, the writer missed by twenty-three words, and these he carried to the empty top margin of page two, just above the three old, deleted lines.

What topics may have been originally mentioned on the discarded page one — what topics and people — there is no way of being sure. The new page with its total of nearly fifty lines, comprising some eight hundred words, treats only a single topic, and treats it in great detail and at length: the bequest to Judith.

On all three pages can be seen smaller changes, words and phrases written in between the lines here and there, the placement indicated by a caret. Twenty such small changes are present (seven on page one, ten on page two, and three on the last page). Of the twenty, however, all but six are mere technical corrections made by Collins or his clerk. The six exceptions have an interest and an underlying significance of their own, for they are traceable to Shakespeare.

None of the six are on page one. Five of them occur on page two. The last, on page three, is the famous line in which the poet leaves to his wife a certain large article of household use, marking the sole reference anywhere in the will to Anne Shakespeare. It occurs near the will's close, written in between lines ten and eleven from the end:

> *Item* I gyve unto my wief my second best bed with the furniture [the bedclothes].

Even in his own plays there may not be a sentence which has managed to call down such an array of critical and biographical comment as those few words. The woman is mentioned in the will only this one time, it is pointed out, and what does she get? A bed, and not even the best one, in a house that must have had a dozen of them. The conclusion of many observers, impressed by the absence of her name elsewhere in the will, is that the poet and his wife had not for a long time seen eye to eye (putting it mildly). Others, more sensibly, reply that the second-best bed was probably the one used by the couple from the start, and in which their three children were conceived and born. They add that a widow, mentioned or not in the will, then had an automatid dower right to one-third of a husband's estate.[1] In reality it was her father's anxiety ofer Judith's future that made reference to the mother so bare.

On the discarded page one, surely, Anne Shakespeare *did* receive the full mention due her from a loving and grateful husband, the usual expression of affection, and with specific mention of her dower right, at least. When the revision of page one, revamping the terms of Judith's bequest, left no room for other matters, Anne obligingly withdrew her own name from the page (we will do her the courtesy of assuming so). But with her favorite bed she was taking no chances, insisting that it must be specified *somewhere* in the will. The spot that Collins found for it was the obvious one, toward the end of page three, just ahead of the more significant bequest of the "broad silver bole" to Judith.

Not so handily can the other five changes inserted by the poet on page two be accounted for, though up to now they have been shrugged off as nothing more than routine. Yet accounted for they certainly can be, and the unraveling moves the riddle of the poet's death another notch closer to a solution.

Three of the five changes are insertions. They add names of friends who were to receive cash for the purchase of memorial rings, a custom of the time (each getting the hefty sum of 26 shillings, eight pence, about a month's wages for a laboring man). Hamnet Sadler and William Reynolds of Stratford, both old friends, were named. Then came three of his London theatre colleagues: the star actor of the old company, Richard Burbage, and two supporting actors, John Heminges and Henry Condell. All five names, it is usually said, were put in as afterthoughts.

Besides friends and colleagues going in, however, one old friend was taken out, his name deleted by a drawn line. Richard Tyler of Stratford, an old schoolfellow of Shakespeare's, was a prosperous merchant and town official, at one time churchwarden of Holy Trinity (his courtship of his wife, it is thought, may have lent some touches to *Romeo and Juliet*). Shakespeare may in fact have been godfather to his son William. If anyone in Stratford deserved to be remembered by the poet with a memorial ring it was Tyler. Yet for some unrecorded reason out came his name, and in its place was entered that of Hamnet Sadler, another old Stratford friend.

The last of the five changes directed by Shakespeare is the most intriguing, for it deprived Judith of a certain item of household goods of considerable value, one appropriate for a bride. "All my Plate" was taken away from Judith and given instead to Shakespeare's eight-year-old granddaughter Elizabeth, the child of Susanna and John Hall. In a mansion the size of New Place, the supply of household plate would have been quite large and expensive, holding in addition to silver and gold pieces many choice items of porcelain, china, and enamelware.

1 Much Shakespeare biography treats Anne harshly, but on no adequate evidence whatever. The latest slam at her (that's the proper word) is in the Greenblatt biography (2004). See Appendix B for a reasoned refutation of Greenblatt's fairly wild charges.

Shakespeare's Will, now preserved in London's Public Record Office (here, much reduced in size). Its two-and-a-half rough, unpunctuated pages show many alterations, insertions, and afterthoughts, prime evidence in solving the puzzle of the poet's death.

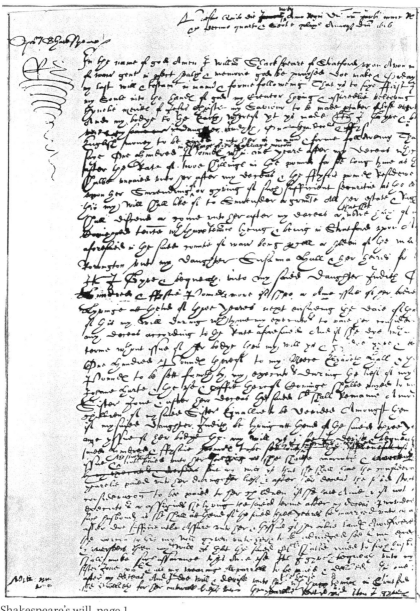

Shakespeare's will, page 1.

Shakespeare's will, page 2.

Shakespeare's will, page 3.

In the altered bequest, however, one exemption was made, an exemption not explained but which in the circumstances proves revealing: one "broad silver & gilt bole," not further described. Evidently this was a large, wide ("broad" to describe a bowl meant very broad), and deep basin of pure silver, its lip or platform or both edged or trimmed in gold. Was the exception made because Judith, on being told by her father that she would not be getting the plate, asked for it as having for her sentimental value? Or did her father make the decision himself to soften the harshness of his action in withholding the one item, the household plate, that should have gone to a newly married, not-quite-so-young daughter? Perhaps it was the latter, for the major change in the will, the rewriting of page one, imposed still harsher conditions on Judith's inheritance.

The big silver-gilt bowl was the way her father and mother chose to make it clear that they still loved her very much, and that it was for her own future good that they were clamping down. Her husband, they were unmistakably saying, could not be trusted.

She still gets three hundred pounds but now it's split in two. One hundred pounds "to discharge her marriage portion" she receives at any time up to a year after her father's death (the executors, Susanna and her husband, to decide when). Another fifty pounds is hers as soon as she surrenders, by written instrument, all her right in a second Shakespeare property in Stratford, a cottage and garden located in Chapel Street across and down a bit from New Place.

The second half of the three hundred pounds is to be tied up in investments, Judith getting the yield only when her husband pays in his promised equivalent of his wife's marriage portion. When he does that, he and Judith are to be given control of the invested money to use as they like. That specification seems clear enough, but the language of the original clause as written has a quite peculiar ring, even apart from the strange Elizabethan spelling and the absence of punctuation:

> Item I gyve and bequeath unto my saied daughter Judith One hundred and ffyftie poundes more if shee or Anie issue of her bodie be lyving att thend of three yeares next ensueing the daie of the date of this my will during which tyme my executours to paie her consideracion from my deceas according to the Rate aforesaid [ten percent] And if she dye within the saied terme without issue of her bodie then my will ys & I doe gyve and bequeath one hundred pounds thereof to my Neece [alternate term for granddaughter] Elizabeth Hall & the ffiftie poundes to be sett forth by my executours during the lief of my sister Johane Hart & the use and proffitt thereof Cominge shalbe paied to my saied sister Jone . . . but if my saied Daughter Judith be lyving at thend of the saied three yeares or anie issue of her bodie then my will ys & so I devise & bequeath the saied hundred and ffiftie poundes to be sett out by my executours and overseers for the best benefitt of her and her

issue & the stock not to be paied unto her so long as shee shalbe marryed & covert Baron [under a husband's protection] but my will ys that shee shall have the consideracion yearelie paied unto her during her lief & after her deceas the saied stock & consideracion to bee paied to her children if shee have anie . . . provided that yf such husbond as shee shall att thend of the saied three yeares be marryed unto or shall attaine after doe sufficientlie Assure unto her & thissue of her bodie landes Awnsereable to the porcion by this my will gyven unto her and to be adjudged soe by my executours & overseers then my will ys that the saied cl pds shalbe paied to such husbond as shall make such assurance to his owne use . . .

What it was in Shakespeare's mind that caused his emphasis on a three-year period — on the eventuality or, it almost seems, the possibility that Judith might die within that time — at the moment escapes knowing. Was it something perhaps buried out of sight in Elizabethan law or custom? Did it perhaps arise out of the poet's own troubled and still veiled thoughts?

Exactly when the wholesale rewrite of Shakespeare's will was done — what month and day of 1616 — proves to be rather easily determined, crucial information in that it helps open the way to the final scene in the hidden drama of the poet's death. (The date affixed to the document itself shows only when it was *signed*, not when it was written.)

In a separate position at the head of page one of the will are two lines of writing which in the day's usual roundabout manner specify the date in Latin. But what it says is by no means clear-cut, in fact it poses a minor riddle of its own. As originally written it reads:

Vicesimo quinto die Januarii Anno Regni Domini Nostri Jacobi nunc regis Anglie etc decimo quarto & Scotie xlix Annoque Domini 1616

The 25th day of January in the reign of King James of England etc., the fourteenth, and of Scotland the 49th, in the year of Our Lord 1616. [punctuation added]

That's the heading on the *rewritten* page one. In itself it indicates that pages two and three, retained unaltered from the original writing, were composed some time earlier. But the heading itself is in error. The fourteenth year of James' reign in England didn't begin until March 24, 1616. Further, for the Elizabethans the legal year began not in January but in March, the 25th day. On January 25th it was still 1615.

Even more curious, at some later time the month of the heading was altered — after the crossed-out *Januarii* the word *Martii* (March) has been inserted. This change corrected both errors in the date-line (as to James' reign and the legal year), and presumably also gave the day on which the instrument was signed (March 25, 1616). The original mistake about the month perhaps resulted, as many have suggested, from an inadvertent carrying over by the clerk or amanuensis of the "January" specified in the first form of page one. The days of the week matching, they needed no alteration.

The existing will, then, was signed on the 25th of March at New Place. In that case, it may be asked, when was page one revised, and when did the meeting occur between Shakespeare and his lawyer in which he ordered the revisions?

Judging by the revisions themselves — severely restricting the bequest to Judith and her husband — the answer has to do with the newly married couple and more particularly with the trouble-prone Thomas. On February 10, 1616, the two were married in Stratford at Holy Trinity Church, of course with both families and many friends attending. Within a week the news was flying around town that Thomas had failed to apply for and get from the local bishop the special license needed to marry at that time of year (a restricted period from mid-January to late March). It was a serious infraction of church law, and he was promptly summoned to a hearing by the Stratford Ecclesiastical Court. He refused to go, was summoned again, and still refused. In his absence the court pronounced a sentence of excommunication against both Quiney and his wife. The date was March 12, 1616.

That same day, but certainly by the 15th, word went speeding round town of the tragic outcome of another of Thomas's embroilments. In giving birth, Margaret Wheeler had died, the baby also being lost. Their deaths occurred on the 12th. On the 15th both mother and baby were buried in Holy Trinity churchyard.

Within days, Thomas was again summoned by the Ecclesiastical Court of Stratford, this time on a charge of fornication ("incontinence") with poor dead Margaret.

At New Place on Friday, March 25, 1616, Shakespeare was shown the completed three-page will. Placing the separate sheets on the table before the poet, Francis Collins offered a quick description of the rewritten page-one contents. Watching as Shakespeare picked up a quill and dipped it in the inkwell were the needed two witnesses, his old Stratford friend and neighbor Julius Shaw and his enigmatic London acquaintance John Robinson. Setting pen to paper, on the right-hand side of the page, after the last sentence of the text halfway down the long sheet, he affixed his signature. As was customary that last sentence read: "In witnesse whereof I have

hereunto put my hand the daie & Yeare first above Written." The word *hand* is written in above the cancelled word *Seale*. That was a momentary slip by Collins. A seal
was the one badge of gentility that Shakespeare still didn't have.

Also at the foot of the text, on the left side of the sheet, Collins wrote, "wit-
nes to the publishing hereof," and then signed his own name. Shaw accepted the
pen, wrote his name under that of Collins, then handed the pen to Robinson, who
signed just beneath Shaw's name. Shakespeare's will was official.

Of course, as a glance at that last page of the will shows (see the illustra-
tion), there are not two witnesses but *four* who signed in addition to Collins. Also,
Shakespeare penned signatures at the bottom of pages one and two as well. Study
of the text yields no proof that the two added witnesses and the extra Shakespeare signatures came at a *later* time, but that, on a careful reading of the evidence, is exactly what happened. In the making of the poet's will, in other words,
there was a third stage, until now unsuspected, which quite certainly is prompted
by the fortunes of a son-in-law proving to be less and less promising.

The two added witnesses — Hamnet Sadler and Robert Whatcott — were
there to attest the five changes made on the *second* page. The first of these completely deprived the Quineys of the very valuable Shakespeare household plate
(all but the silver gilt bowl). The next four recognize, by a gift of memorial rings,
some of the poet's personal friends in Stratford and London — but for one of those
friends there is the peremptory cancellation or rescinding of that recognition.

Stricken out is the affluent, politically well-connected Richard Tyler. In his
place is entered the old reliable Hamnet Sadler. Newly added is William Reynolds,
whose impressive Stratford mansion stood near the Avon river. a half-mile from
New Place. Also new are the actors Burbage, Heminges, and Condell.

The rejected Tyler — so suggests the whole tendency of the evidence — fell
from grace and was taken out of the will for one reason only: when requested by
Shakespeare to act on behalf of the endangered Thomas Quiney, he declined. His
position and contacts he could have used to forestall or get thrown out the serious case pending against the young man in the church court. But apparently he
wouldn't, not even for an old friend. Sadler and Reynolds, on the other hand — so
again says the evidence — were put in because, acceding to Shakespeare's earnest
request, they did act for Quiney, and what is more, did so successfully. Their efforts saved Quiney from a court sentence of unusual harshness, one which would
have imposed on him as punishment a humbling act, one of utter public humiliation, very much peculiar to the times.

On March 26, 1616, before the Vicar of Holy Trinity and other officials of town
and church, Thomas Quiney was charged with having had criminal sexual relations ("carnal copulation") with the woman Margaret Wheeler, spinster, and un-
lawfully getting her with child (thus being in some measure, it is implied but not
stated, responsible for her death). Quiney, it seems, did not dissemble, but openly

and readily confessed his guilt and "submitted himself to the correction of the court." In the firm view of the era, penance for sins of the flesh required a public demonstration, both to purge guilt and to express a wish to be forgiven. Its most devastating form was a dramatic exhibition in church, a display of sorrow and contrition before the assembled congregation at a Sunday service. Completely draped from head to toe in an enveloping white sheet, the penitent had to stand silent and unmoving on a platform at the head of the center aisle from the start of the service to the end. This was the sentence given Quiney, not for one Sunday only, but for three.

As it turned out, however, Stratfordians, all agog over a scandal in the home of the famous author, didn't get to see the promised spectacle in their church. Soon after its decision was announced, the court without explanation reduced the sentence. Now it was deemed sufficient if Quiney paid a fine, a large one at five shillings, and personally appeared before the minister of the nearby village of Bishopton, "to acknowledge the fault in his own attire." He must then certify his compliance to the next session of the church court.

The original handwritten minutes of the Quiney session of the Ecclesiastical court still exist, a brief thirteen-line entry on a page with two other cases. But about them there is something quite peculiar, that is, about their location. They are in a minute-book where they don't belong.

The surviving records of the Stratford Ecclesiastical Court — popular opinion knew it as the "Bawdy Court" — are contained in two oversized ledgers, all the others having been lost. One is of 74 pages, the other of 70, both volumes measuring seven by twelve inches. The first covers cases heard in the years between 1590 and 1608, the second runs for only three years, 1622-1624. The peculiarity is that the Quiney session, though it was held on March 25, 1616, is entered in the first volume. Strangely, it occupies a leaf between two sessions of 1608.

No one has explained how or why the misplaced entry happened, how it found its way into a ledger completed eight years before, when it should have appeared in a third volume (or a fourth) between the existing two. A further interesting fact, in itself not so peculiar, is that the two surviving ledgers are no longer in Stratford. Now they repose in the Record Office, Maidstone, in the county of Kent, far to the south of Warwickshire.

From beginning to end the handwritten text of Shakespeare's will is entirely bare of punctuation. Decidedly, such a downright threat to clarity in a document conveying valuable assets was *not*, as some have claimed, a feature of Elizabethan legal practice.

While containing some 1500 words (equal to five or six typed pages, double-spaced), not a period, comma, colon, semi-colon, dash, or other mark is to be seen, nothing to break up and slow down the thought carried along by the flood of language. Nor is there in the three pages any slightest attempt at paragraphing. In line after line the words, with scarcely a separation between them or only the narrowest, slide along unhindered. Add to these defects, surprising enough in themselves, the many deletions, the interlined additions, the at times obscure or incomplete phrasing, the sloppy handwriting in general, and the occasional blurring or spotting of the ink (quite noticeable in some twenty lines), and the truth dawns. The Shakespeare will as it exists is not a finished instrument meant for the client to sign. It is a corrected draft. In effect mere worksheets, the three pages as they now appear were *never* intended to serve as a fair copy, an official document ready for signing.

Yet no fair copy was made, and this draft with all its imperfections *was* signed by the poet. Why?

The answer begins with a close look at the signatures themselves, as written on each page by the poet's own hand. The first one — at the foot of page one in the left margin — is now much faded and fragmented, almost if not completely unreadable. But it was copied and published long ago, so is still viewable in nearly pristine form.

The first reaction of most people to the three signatures is that two of them, those on pages one and two, are very sloppily written. They suggest, in fact, a hand for some reason grown unsteady. That conclusion is not a new one but has been voiced by any number of qualified observers: the hand that traced the name *William Shakspere* on pages one and two, attesting the various small changes in the text, definitely seems to have been somehow impaired. The third signature, written on the last page in affirmation of the entire document, has not been judged in the same light, not seen as defective. More than just the name, in unfaded ink it reads, "By me William Shakspere." Except perhaps for the elaborate capital B, so puzzling to unprepared modern eyes, the four words set off by themselves are still easily readable.

However, the third signature, too, was quite definitely written by a hand in some way enfeebled. It is the presence of the initial words, "By me William," that masks the reality. Those three words, isolated and studied separately, indeed show themselves to be well and firmly written, having no sign of debility. But the "Shakspere" — looked at closely on its own under magnification and in comparison with the neat "William" — uncovers the revealing truth. The first three words were written by Collins (or his clerk). Only the trembling, off-line *Shakspere* came from the poet's pen. (See the enlargement on p. 27.)

Nor is it difficult to determine, almost to the day, when each of the three Shakespeare signatures was written.

Immediately on hearing of his son-in-law's double misfortune in mid-March (his excommunication and the Wheeler affair which brought a summons from the Bawdy Court), Shakespeare ordered the wholesale rewrite of page one, limiting Judith's bequest. Soon completed was the makeshift revision, but the making .of the fair copy was delayed, and it still wasn't ready when on March 25th an anxious Shakespeare was allowed to sign his name to the last page of the draft, his hand shaking as he wrote. It was a few days after the signing, say two or three, following a flurry of behind-the-scenes maneuvering, that Thomas Quiney's sentencing by the Bawdy Court was reduced to a milder, much more private penance, imposing no public humiliation.

With that, in early April — say three weeks before his death — the relieved Shakespeare again sent for his lawyer. Not naming his reasons, he proceeded to drop from his will the name of the uncooperative Richard Tyler, now no longer a friend, and adding in its place the names of Sadler and Reynolds, the two who'd managed to arrange things for young Quiney with the Bawdy Court. Attesting these changes he now signed page two. At Collins' suggestion he also signed page one, the solicitor feeling that it wouldn't do to leave one of the three sheets unacknowledged by the testator.

It was at this time that the extraneous witnesses, numbers four and five, were called in to vouch for the latest small changes in the will. Hamnet Sadler, who lived close by, and the enigmatic Robert Whatcott, the same man who'd come to the defense of Susanna Hall three years earlier, signed one after another just below the three earlier witnesses.

The resulting column of names creates the visually misleading impression that all five men signed as witnesses at the same time. (Study of the ink seems to show that three different inks were involved: one for Collins, another for Shaw and Robinson, still another for the last two names.)

But if all this is true, then the brief description given in the above pages of that first, formal signing of the will on March 25th certainly cannot be a full and faithful picture of all that actually happened that spring day at New Place. The questions prompting such a conclusion are obvious:

Why would Shakespeare ask to sign a rough, a very rough draft of his will, rather than wait the short time needed to prepare a fair copy? The writing out of the ninety lines with punctuation inserted and phrasing finalized would have occupied Collins or his clerk barely an hour, at most two if any doubts or questions had arisen.

Why did Collins, an experienced lawyer, allow his client to sign such a sorry legal document as this hurried, sloppily written draft? Certainly it didn't reflect well on him professionally. If his clerk wasn't available he might easily have done the copying himself or paid some Stratford amanuensis to do it, several of whom no doubt were located a few minutes' walk from his office.

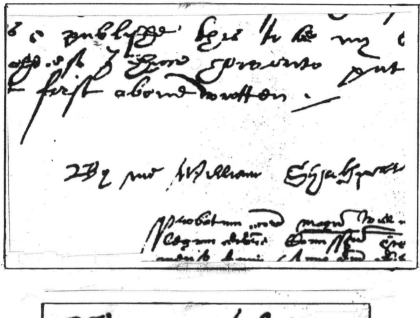

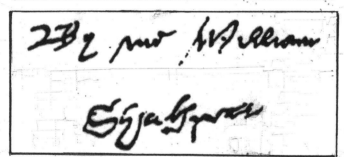

Fig. 6: (top) Shakespeare's signature on the third (last) page of his will. It is preceded by the phrase "By me." The elaborate script of the time makes it hard for modern eyes to follow, for instance the Capital B in "By." (bottom) Further enlargement of the two names, *William* and *Shakspeare,* clearly shows that each came from a different hand. The first is steady and controlled, the other shaky and enfeebled, barely able to complete the word.

But there are many wills of the day, it is said, showing somewhat similar clerical and technical defects, improprieties which didn't bar successful probate. Yet as others have replied, no one can point to another Elizabethan will that includes so full and embarrassing a catalog of such deficiencies, all of which could have been cleaned up by an hour's copying.

The truth is — must be — that there wasn't an hour to spare, nor any part of an hour.

In reality, the signing of the will on March 25, 1616, it may be concluded, was conducted in a setting of great hurry and commotion, in fact amidst considerable excitement, likely affecting both family and servants.

When Shakespeare, his hand quivering, picked up the feathered quill that day and, after the neatly written "By me William", painstakingly traced the nine wavering letters of "Shakspere," he was, or thought he was, a dying man, each moment threatening to be his last.

3.
THE REPLINGHAM NOTE

Anne Shakespeare, née Hathaway, was in a certain sense among the unluckiest of women. Married for almost thirty-four years to one of the true immortals, a man whose name is celebrated around the world, instead of occupying a proper niche of her own as the consort of greatness, she remains faceless, characterless, a largely unknown quantity.

It was a pure accident of historical timing, of course, along with the uncertain flow of circumstance, that robbed her of her rightful place in history, a place perhaps much higher than anyone has suspected. Who knows but that it was Anne's love and encouragement that gave young Will the strength to leave home and family and front the daunting whirl of the London playhouses. It might well have been her faith in and understanding of his genius that made him believe in himself long before he had any tangible reason to do so (the situation that confronts every hopeful artist just starting out).

At least that possibility should be raised, should be kept steadily in mind — as it never is — if for no other reason than to offset the two lone facts that are known about her, and always emphasized: she was eight years older than her husband (26 to his 18 when they married), and she bore her first child, Susanna, six months after the wedding.

A few other facts about Anne are derivable by inference. For example, before and after moving into the Chapel Street house, except for the company of her two daughters, for many years she found herself much of the time alone. During most of each year the business of acting and writing kept her husband in London or on the road (memorizing parts, incessant rehearsals, frequent performances, script revisions and additions) in what amounted to a repertory company that seldom gave the same play more than once or twice in succession in the same place. What original writing he did would have been fitted into odd moments and the silent, lonely hours late at night, when he also no doubt thought longingly of his comfortable home and loving family. His visits back to Stratford could only have been widely spaced, say two or three times a year, and a bit more depending on the company's movements and commitments. Looking after her two girls, aged fourteen and twelve when they first moved into New Place, and running a large and unfamiliar establishment with, surely, no fewer than a half-dozen servants as well as cook and a gardener (a large and heavily planted garden stretched far out behind the house), kept Anne busy in Stratford. No visits by her and the girls to London are recorded, but there must have been at least an annual rite of such trips, probably occupying several weeks at a time. How else would they get to see those new plays of Will's that everybody was talking about, see them under the best conditions, which would be at the Globe?

Being on her own, however, didn't mean that Anne was lonely for companionship. Literally she was surrounded by close family, on both sides, allowing her small chance to moon over an absent spouse. Two streets over lived the Shakespeares, mother, father, a married sister with her children, and three unmarried brothers, all still occupying the rambling old home in Henley Street. Her own family, the Hathaways, was also nearby, mother, sisters, brothers, aunts, uncles, nieces and nephews, living in both Stratford and Shottery. In her big house Anne didn't lack for daily visitors, no doubt frequently including overnight guests.

Still, comforting as it was to know that loving hearts were just around the corner, it wasn't the same as having somebody living in the house, and at length more permanent residents did arrive. Thomas Greene of Warwick was a distant cousin of Shakespeare's, probably by marriage rather than by blood. Married and in his early thirties, with his wife, Letitia, about 1603 he came to Stratford to take up an appointment as Town Solicitor, later becoming Town Clerk. By profession a lawyer, he was also a practicing poet, with high artistic ambitions of his own. In the life of his famous cousin, it seems, he filled a role not previously understood, that of protégé. No other reason, in fact no reason at all, has been suggested for his presence at New Place. In Shakespeare biography the fact itself gets barely passing mention, often with the comment that the poet when away no doubt felt easier having a man on the premises.

An enigmatic figure, this Greene. With his wife and their three children — two of them named Anne and William, born at New Place — he lived with the Shakespeares for some seven years, perhaps as many as nine (the year he moved in is uncertain). He was there during the momentous period when three of the four great tragedies were written (*Othello*, *Lear*, and *Macbeth*), as well as many other plays, perhaps a few of the sonnets. Outside of Shakespeare's own family, no one enjoyed such sustained intimacy with the poet as did Thomas Greene, no one had such an opportunity to gather knowledge of the playwright and his work. Yet, though he outlived his benefactor by more than twenty years, he wrote nothing at all about his unparalleled experience, said nothing, told nothing. He did, however, while he was living at New Place, write and publish a sonnet offering high praise of another contemporary poet, a friend and rival of Shakespeare's, Michael Drayton. His own career as a poet went nowhere, a failure which resulted at least to some extent from his decision, once he reached Stratford, to concentrate on more worldly rewards. In this he succeeded admirably.

Greene's lengthy residence at New Place ended with or just before the retirement and return home of Shakespeare in 1611. With his family he moved to another house he'd purchased in town, but still keeping up his link with the poet, now more in his capacity of lawyer and town clerk. When in 1614 the threat of land enclosure loomed in Stratford, he was at the center of the resulting storm. On behalf of the Town Council — an arrangement carefully set down in writing — by legal means and social pressure he vigorously opposed the moneyed enclosure interests, hoping to permanently halt the move. First, though, like Shakespeare, he assured himself by written agreement with the same moneyed enclosers, that his own considerable investment in the affected lands would be protected no matter who won.

In Stratford's enclosure affair Thomas Greene played a curious double role. In the end it cost him the friendship and good will of the man who for so many years had given him a home. The one name that should appear in Shakespeare's will, aside from family members, is that of Thomas Greene.

It isn't there.

Behind closed doors, in the private study of Shakespeare at New Place, six men sat talking. Besides the poet himself, there were three experienced lawyers. One, named William Replingham, was there as official representative of the Enclosers (a small group headed by the hugely wealthy Combe brothers, William and Thomas, and the influential Arthur Mainwaring, steward to England's Lord Chancellor). The other two lawyers, Thomas Lucas and his associate Michael Olney (husband of Anne Shakespeare's goddaughter, Anne Parsons), were there to act on behalf of Shakespeare. Called in to serve as witnesses were the Reverend John Rogers, Vicar of Holy Trinity (whose house in Chapel Lane was only yards from New Place), and a family friend, Anthony Nash (whose son in 1626 would marry Shakespeare's granddaughter, Elizabeth Hall).

The date of the meeting was October 28, 1614. The doors of the study were closed because neither of the principal parties, Replingham and Shakespeare, cared to have it known that they were about to conclude an arrangement which, in effect, would buy the poet's silence in the fight that was sure to come over enclosure. Eliminating a potential opponent, the Combes and Mainwaring had decided, one able to wield considerable influence and who could bring strong pressures to bear behind the scenes, was worth whatever it might cost to indemnify his losses. In prior discussions it had been agreed that specific sums couldn't be fixed so early, both sides admitting, however, that the annual losses could grow to be quite substantial. In addition to being one of the larger landholders in the proposed area just north of town, Shakespeare was also part owner of the town tithes, a large investment he'd made some years before. His annual return on the tithes rose and fell with fluctuation of property values and rental fees, an unstable situation that was an inevitable result of enclosure.

From a case Replingham drew a two-page document, one side of each sheet covered with writing. He laid it on the table before Shakespeare, explaining that he thought it was broad enough to cover all contingencies. The number of referees it stipulated — four "indifferent persons" to be chosen and agreed on by both sides — was only slightly unusual in such cases. Joining their client at the table, Lucas and Olney read along with him, beginning with the date in Latin. The two parties were specified as "William Shackespeare, of Stratford in the County of Warwick, gent.," and "William Replingham, of Great Harborough in the County of Warwick, gent." (A relative of Mainwaring's, in order to back up his position as front man in this agreement, Replingham would of course have had a separate contract with Mainwaring and the Combes.)

Carefully the opening paragraphs list the Shakespeare acreage to the north of town: parcels in Gospel Bush, Bishopton, Ford's Green, the Dingles, and Welcombe, with some smaller scattered pieces. Specified for each location were the present values and the expected annual yield, noting highs and lows. It is in the final paragraph that the obligation of the Enclosers is expressed (the spelling is here modernized):

> ...the said William Replingham, his heirs or assigns, shall, upon reasonable request, satisfy, content and make recompense unto him, the said William Shackespeare or his assigns, for all such loss, detriment and hindrance as he, the said William Shackespeare, his heirs and assigns, shall or may be thought, in the view and judgment of four indifferent persons, to be indifferently elected by the said William and William, and their heirs, and in default of the said William Replingham, by the said William Shackespeare or his heirs only, to survey and judge the same, to sustain or incur for or in respect of the decreasing of the yearly value of the tithes by reason of any enclosure or decay of tillage there meant and intended by the said William Replingham; and that the said William Replingham and his heirs shall procure such sufficient security unto the said William Shackespeare and his heirs, for the performance of this covenant as shall be devised by learned Counsel...[1]

Beginning with Replingham, each of the six wrote his signature at the bottom of the page. Why the attestation of the two lawyers was added, when the two witnesses

[1] Readers who are familiar with this document will have spotted what seems an error of omission. To spare them needless concern I'll state here that a sufficient explanation will appear presently.

Nash and Rogers would have been enough, isn't clear. On its face the document was fairly straightforward. Only in its background, the peculiar circumstances lurking behind it, was there something about its character to be questioned.

It was two weeks later, at an unplanned meeting in London, that Shakespeare learned for the first time that the town's fight against enclosure would be led by his former protégé and house-guest, Thomas Greene. A knowledgeable and highly competent lawyer with important contacts in the London courts (he was a graduate of the Middle Temple), Greene had been selected for his vital role by the Stratford Council, perhaps also in part because he was himself a tithe-owner, so had good reason to oppose enclosure. Actually his purchase of a tithe-portion, back in 1609, had been done in some secrecy, annoying and to an extent alarming various Council members. He had, it was charged, "deceived and dealt evilly with us in buying of one Humphry Coles, Esquire, an interest in tithes the inheritance whereof is in us." Other members, though, rose in his defense, dismissing the charge as having been made by "unknown authors" and certifying that the Town Clerk "for his fidelity and endeavours in our behalf always used us very well."

In asking Greene to head up its legal battle with the Enclosers the Stratford Council made clear, by means of a separate written agreement, its reason for choosing him: their faith in his integrity and ability, not merely because of his position as Town Clerk. The agreement no doubt also guaranteed his expenses for the necessary London trips to attend court, and perhaps in addition specified a salary, at least some sort of monetary reward.

In London on November 16, 1614, as Greene himself notes, Shakespeare, with Dr. Hall his son-in-law, met with Greene, who was making his initial moves in court regarding enclosure. "At my cosen Shakespeare coming yesterday to town," he wrote that evening, "I went to see him how he did," the meeting taking place perhaps at Shakespeare's new house in Blackfriars or perhaps at the Globe Theatre. It wasn't all that casual a visit just to "see how he did," however, but concerned itself mainly with the serious and growing threat to Stratford's common lands.

Again according to Greene's own notes, Shakespeare had quite a bit to say on the topic, imparting what seemed rather significant insider information. The extent of the planned enclosure, he informed his townsman, had been a good deal cut back. Now the designated land would reach no further than Clopton's place, from "Gospel Bush, and so up straight, leaving out part of the Dingles, to the Field, then to the gate in Clopton hedge, taking in Salisbury's piece."

But for another five or so months, the poet added, nothing at all would be done. The needed surveys wouldn't begin until spring, late April or May. Only after that would the actual ditching start along the boundaries of the specified territory, and the planting of hedges as fencing. It was even possible that the entire project would be abandoned, finished Shakespeare, the Combes deciding that the

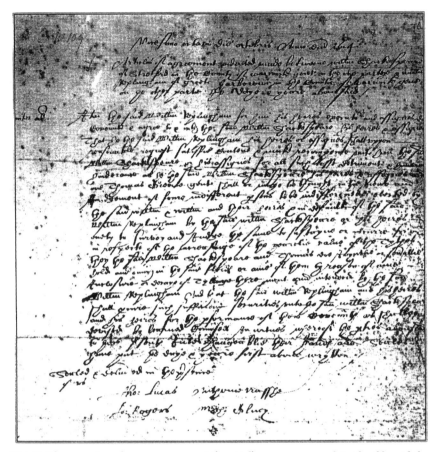

Fig. 7: The secret enclosure agreement (partial), now preserved in the files of the Shakespeare Trust, Stratford. As Shakespeare wished, the original agreement was destroyed. But one paragraph from the document was copied and preserved by hostile hands in Stratford.

expected gain wasn't worth a protracted battle and giving up in disgust ("he and Mr. Hall say they think there will be nothing done at all").

To all that the two men told him Greene listened respectfully. But even as he listened he was all too aware that they were mistaken, that everything they said about the enclosure was in error. Only the day before this London meeting with Shakespeare and Dr. Hall, Greene had been in consultation, also in London, with none other than William Replingham, the Enclosers' agent. They were now, it appeared, making a play for their chief opponent, hoping to neutralize him as they had several others including Shakespeare. Revealingly, the meeting took place, not indoors but in the tumultuous privacy of one of central London's busiest streets. Greene's note of it manages to hint strongly at much more than it states:

> Against Whitehall Wall I met with Master Replingham, who promised to come to me in the afternoon, saying I should be satisfied. I asked him how the town should be satisfied, and he answered he cared not for their consents.

There would be no reduction in the original extent of the enclosures, Greene knew, whatever Shakespeare thought. Further, the indispensable land surveys would not by any means be delayed to spring. In fact, as he no doubt learned from Replingham that same evening, at that very moment back home the surveyors were already at work, with completion of the job expected within weeks. Weather permitting, the ditching and hedging would be underway by early December.

It took Greene three more weeks to surrender to the Enclosers, a move he made after going home to Stratford to discover how hopeless now seemed the fight. By mid-December a large party of diggers was busily at work building the enclosures, and proceeding so rapidly that the hedging went up at the rate of some three hundred feet per week. Greene's last traceable official act on behalf of the Council's campaign against the Enclosers took place on December 23, 1614, when the discouraged members sent letters to certain pivotal figures asking that the town's welfare be put above the that of the moneyed classes. Two of the more important letters went to Arthur Mainwaring, who if he wished could directly affect matters, and to William Shakespeare, the one resident whose personal influence, as both famed author and wealthy townsman, might by itself turn the tide. "Letters written," reads a Greene jotting, "one to Mr. Mainwaring another to Mr. Shakespeare with almost all the company's [the Council] hands to either. I also writ of myself to cousin Shakespeare, the copies of all our oathes made then, also a note of the inconveniences that would grow by the Enclosure."

Both letters, it seems, went out laden with nearly all twenty-one signatures of the earnest Council members. Stressed in each, besides the obvious baleful effects on the general population to be expected from enclosure, was the inevitable drastic drop in town revenues. Such a dwindling of public monies pointedly stated the letters, would bring ruin on the borough, "wherein live about seven hundred poor which receive alms, whose curses and clamours will be daily poured out to God against the enterprisers of such a thing."

From neither man came any response, in the eyes of the Council hardly surprising as to Mainwaring, but downright puzzling as to the usually generous, kind-hearted poet. At this juncture no one outside of a small circle knew anything of the Replingham Note, none knew that this time Shakespeare had decided in favor of his own long-held dream of building an estate and founding a family line. He also had on his side, it must be said, the probability of a positive future good, one which would at first work severe hardship for many but which would at last prove beneficial for all. The old medieval system for use of the common lands, held so tenaciously by the people, had become wasteful of both land and labor, employing and encouraging outworn methods of agriculture. Most often, though it would take years to prove itself, enclosure was a firm step into the future.

The threat of actual violence was soon in the air. In December a delegation to the Combes from the town Council was turned back with a sneer and a warning that they'd find themselves in an unequal struggle with some of the country's most important men. To their faces the delegates were called "dogs and curs," and William Combe, on being warned that the town might take direct action to halt the hedging, responded "in a threatening manner with very great passion and anger."

On January 9th some brief, if ugly fighting did break out at the hedging operation as several Stratfordians tried to halt the digging. While the "riotous disorder" was in progress, William Combe on horseback happened to come along. Pulling up, he sat in the saddle laughing loudly at the way his workers manhandled their irate attackers, one burly individual threatening to bury his opponent "in the bottom of the ditch." Then, two days later, a mob of women and children under cover of darkness slipped out of town, went to the site and began rooting up the hedges already in place.

The situation was ripe for real harm, when on February 28th the London courts finally acted, granting an injunction which forbade the enclosures to proceed pending further notice. Then on April 2nd at the Warwick Assizes the court handed down its final decision on the still-boiling controversy. Against all expectation, it declared a permanent prohibition on the Enclosers, ordering them to desist immediately. Under threat of large fines and imprisonment, they were told to drop all plans affecting the common lands, and to forthwith remove all obstructions.

No one on either side really believed it was over, and it wasn't. But for Thomas Greene it no longer mattered. By then he'd been "satisfied" by the Enclosers. He'd had several private meetings with them and as a result his name was added to the Shakespeare-Replingham note. Two small, unobtrusive interlineations did the deed. Now whichever way it went, Greene was safe against loss.

In the curious sheaf of notes kept by Thomas Greene covering the first fifteen months of the enclosure affair, one brief passage occurs which has alternately intrigued and puzzled investigators, nobody knowing quite what to make of it, if anything is to be made. As a result, the seventeen words of the passage now generally draw only a dismissive comment or two. Yet when it is read in a certain context, the simple statement, of no apparent significance, yields quite a special relevance indeed.

On the page in question they occupy two lines, not as part of the sequence of other notes but set off by themselves, inserted into a blank space on the right-hand side of the page between two paragraphs:

> Sept Mr Shakespeares telling J Greene that I was not able to bear the enclos-ing of Welcombe

John Greene was Thomas's brother, his associate in the town clerk's office. Why, asks one commentator after another, should Shakespeare tell John something he must already have known, at least probably knew, that enclosure would work an economic hardship on Thomas? If Shakespeare did make such an apparently aimless comment, why should John relay it to Thomas, and why should Thomas bother making a note of it?

What was it in or about the remark itself that *needed* saying, and by an out-sider to John? What was it in or about the remark that caught the attention of its object, to whom there could have been nothing new in the information?

The explanation favored by many is a fairly convoluted one, not to say free-wheeling, which begins in part by rewriting the passage. The "I," it is suggested, is actually a badly written or incomplete "he," a change which transposes the sen-tence into an outright declaration by the poet that he was against enclosure, that he personally could not "bear" it. The same result is achieved by those who see the whole phrase — "I was not able to bear the enclosing of Welcombe" — as a direct quote, without the marks, from Shakespeare's own lips in which he declares for the common man's side in the vexed question. Either way is acceptable to most Shakespeare scholars, since both tend to relieve the poet of the seeming selfish-ness of his contract with the Enclosers.

But the first of these interpretations is quite denied by close analysis of the "I," which is seen as being exactly what it purports to be (a conclusion supported by experts). The second interpretation cannot on its face be either proved or dis-proved, of course, leaving the decision to each individual. Still there are few even among scholars who think it likely.

Other suggestions are more general. One focusses on a tiny squiggle preced-ing the word "bear," which is crossed out and which appears to form the letters "he . . ." This might indicate that the word *help* (in the sense of *prevent*), was first intended, the writer changing his mind as he wrote. Another sees the word "bear" as a stumble of the writer, who meant instead to scribble *bar* (of course spelled more like *barre* in those times). Each of these interpretations radically alters the meaning of the passage, while leaving the writer in place as its object.

As so often with such historico-literary puzzles, however, no revisionary approaches are necessary. It is *context* which determines here. Once that is known there's no need to go beyond the clear surface meaning of the words.

The Replingham note: *that* is the obviously relevant context. The private nature of the document, and its questionable purpose, for both Shakespeare and Greene, are the crux, or to express it concisely, the secret *at the time* of its existence.

The original of the Replingham note no longer exists, at least has not been found. What does survive is a contemporary copy of its final portion, the paragraph setting out the responsibility of the Enclosers. It was made by Greene himself, and was for long in his possession (its earlier clauses, listing the Shakespeare properties around Welcombe, had no particular interest or application for him). The significant thing about it is that the two insertions adding his name as a beneficiary are now (in this copy) *within* the text, as if originally written there. The first insertion is short, following a stipulation as to Shakespeare's heirs and assigns in line seven: "and one Thomas Greene, gent." The second is longer, occupying lines thirteen/fourteen, and, curiously, seem to say that Greene and the poet were in some sense and degree partners in ownership of at least a few parcels of land. Again, the insertion follows a stipulation as to Shakespeare: "and Thomas doe joyntly or severallie hold and enjoy in the said fieldes, or anie of them."

Both insertions betray their extraneous and almost hurried nature as afterthoughts by being bare of all further identification of Greene, as well as the lack of any reference to his "heirs and assignes." Against Shakespeare's name the phrase occurs a half-dozen times, as it would normally.

In light of such facts, certain questions become urgent: when and by whom was Greene's name added to the Replingham note? More pertinently, *why*? Surprisingly, all these questions can be readily answered.

The name was added on one of three days in January 1615, the 9th, 10th, or 11th. The insertion followed an emergency meeting of the Stratford Council a few days earlier, held to consider the town's legal position, now that actual hedging — the definitive act in the enclosure process — had begun, causing violence. The pen was wielded by Thomas Lucas, Shakespeare's attorney, of course with the poet's consent, and that of the Enclosers. As with Shakespeare, the two simple additions to the original text effectively bought Greene's silence.

The decision to join his opponents was reached by Greene after a visit to his home by William Combe, who boldly proposed a bribe. First, a figure of ten pounds was mentioned, but only as a mere proffer of a much larger sum for full cooperation, mainly the influencing of others (for instance, Sir Henry Rainsford of the nearby village of Clifford Chambers). The imperious Combe, noted Greene, "after many promises and protestations that I should be well dealt withal, departed, and I brought him to the door."

A day or two later Replingham himself showed up as a supper guest at the Greene home. With him he brought the original Shakespeare agreement made the previous October 28. Repeating Combe's assurances that he should be "well dealt withal," as Greene watched he wrote in the two additions, between the lines. Then, while Replingham no doubt had his dinner, Greene made his personal copy of the operative clause — certainly over Replingham's objections. Concluded in secret, not at any time to be made public, the agreement didn't allow for or contemplate the making of uncontrolled copies, not even in part. But when Greene showed himself adamant, Replingham reluctantly gave in.

It was a mistake, and a grievous one. Exactly the outcome that Shakespeare had feared would follow from public knowledge of what he'd done in joining the Enclosers, happened. Admittedly the evidence for that conclusion is indirect. But when studied it proves in some ways hardly less forceful than if it were contained in a signed confession.

When, many years later, the copy made by Greene was unearthed, it turned up in, of all unexpected places, the official town archives of Stratford. No one can say how it got there, no one can say when — except for the fact that Thomas Greene left Stratford for good in the early spring of 1617, less than a year after Shakespeare's death. Sometime, then, between *that* date and January 1615, when the copy was made — two years and a bit more — the Greene copy of the Replingham note's final, tell-tale paragraph found its way to a shelf among the town's public records, where it lay open to all inquisitive eyes. Whether it was Greene himself who deposited it there, or someone to whom he may have given it, is beside the point. Either way, it can be said with full justice that it was the poet's former protégé who for no known reason, on purpose or by inadvertence, broke his secret.

To that fact add this:

In the hundred years after Shakespeare's death, Stratfordians made no official move to honor his memory: no resolutions of regret and sorrow were passed on his demise, no special ceremonies were held at his funeral, no monuments created in the town's streets or public buildings, nothing done to preserve or notice his work, name, or fame. While the Shakesperean literary achievement — after mid-century, say — began fast gathering recognition elsewhere, in the official circles of his hometown, his birthplace, it was quietly and completely ignored.

The minor puzzle created by Greene's cryptic jotting in his enclosure diary about Shakespeare, himself, and his brother John, now unravels. When he scribbled, in the blank space between two unrelated paragraphs, the words, "Mr Shakespeares telling J Green that I was not able to bear the enclosing of Welcombe," he meant just what the plain words say. He meant that the poet was explaining to John, in response to a question, the reason *why* Thomas's name had been added to the Replingham note.

Fig. 8: The Shakespeare residence in Stratford. Here with his wife Anne and two daughters (a son died young) he lived for some twenty years when not in London or on the road. Among the town's most elegant houses, it had a huge garden at the t he back. An earlier, rougher sketch gives it five gables. It was taken down in 1759.

In September 1615, as the Enclosure imbroglio cooled down for the moment, John Greene learned for the first time of the note's existence, and his brother's inclusion in it. He was surprised to find that his upright brother and the sympathetic poet should, in secret, have played such a double-handed game of self-interest, especially his brother who'd already signed an agreement to use his best efforts on behalf of the town Council.

Shakespeare's explanation in reply to John's inquiry touched not himself, but only his co-beneficiary. If Thomas had failed to take steps, said Shakespeare, he would after enclosure have found himself in total financial ruin. It was in this obvious sense that Greene "was not able to bear" the reshuffling of Stratford's common lands.

Fig. 9: This life-size statue of Shakespeare, in Stratford's public park, shows him elegantly attired in the fashion of a "gentleman," then an official designation. Seconding that elevated status was his reputation as one of the day's leading poets and playwrights, a dual role that meant a great deal to him.

Before the able and evidently worldly-wise town clerk of Stratford is allowed to leave the stage, one or two other interesting facts about him need to be listed. Thomas Greene, it appears, had curious if tangential links to both of the recent ugly episodes touching Shakespeare's family, the one affecting his elder daughter, the other his younger girl and her husband.

The young man, John Lane, who was charged with spreading the rumor about Susanna's infidelity, was a relative of Greene's by marriage. Margaret Lane, John's sister, had in 1609 married John Greene, Thomas's brother, so the malicious rumor-spreader certainly was known to Greene on a personal basis. What part Greene may have played in the unpleasant — or, better, say the harrowing — incident of 1613 has never been investigated. Common sense, surely, may conclude that once Lane's identity was known, Greene would have been among the first to be approached by Susanna's shocked and angry father.

Actually the tales told about Susanna's moral laxity, successfully combatted in court if not put wholly to rest, in reality were far more damaging to the woman and her family than has appeared. The phrase specified in court as having been used by Lane — that Susanna "had the runninge of the raynes" — was almost a mortal blow. Always it is taken to mean that Hall's wife was a bossy woman in the home, in all things dictating and dominating the management of domestic and family affairs, a not unreasonable conclusion. But it had nothing whatever to do with the home. In that day's jargon, "runninge of the raynes" referred to a sexually transmitted disease (about this there is no doubt, for Dr. Hall himself in his medical records uses the phrase).

John Lane in spreading his disgraceful story was actually saying — and all who heard the phrase would have understood — that Mistress Hall in her extramarital escapades had contracted gonorrhea. Most who heard the charge would have promptly made the leap to the fact of Susanna's seeming barrenness during the preceding six or so years. After the birth of her daughter Elizabeth in February 1608 there had been no more pregnancies.

Perhaps even more disturbing for Shakespeare than Greene's link to the Hall-Lane episode was his connection with the Quiney-Wheeler case, this one a blood connection.

In March 1616 Thomas Quiney, husband of Judith Shakespeare, stood before the Stratford Ecclesiastical tribunal (the Bawdy Court) accused of fornication with the perished Margaret Wheeler, getting her with child, the baby also dying. He was there in the first place because according to the regular procedure, he'd been named to the court ("cited") as an offender by the court's "apparitor," a functionary whose task it was to root out and report evildoers. In the Quiney case the Apparitor was an obscure town official by the name of Richard Greene.

This was the third of the three Greene brothers, originally of Warwick, now residents of Stratford, the other two being John and Thomas. Though he is not mentioned as such in the town records, Richard Greene, Apparitor of the Ecclesiastical Court, was the younger brother of Shakespeare's friend and former protégé, Thomas Greene.

When Shakespeare first heard that his son-in-law had been cited to the Bawdy Court he would also have known who did the citing: a cousin of his own, the brother of the man he had for years sheltered at New Place and to whom he'd willingly given encouragement as a writer, a man who had lived with him almost as one of the family . . .

Picture what happened at New Place on the day the court summons arrived for young Quiney, then living there with Judith.

Picture the face of the stricken poet when he came into the room and was told of his son-in-law's impending disgrace, perhaps told by the tearful, trembling Judith herself.

Picture him at his desk furiously scribbling a note, then calling loudly for a messenger to carry the note to the Apparitor's brother, Thomas, in his house down near the river.

Fig. 10: Shakespeare's granddaughter Elizabeth, Lady Barnard of Abington and Stratford. Eight years old when her grandfather died, she inherited by a curious and revealing last-minute change in his will the family's large and expensive collection of "household Plate." Married twice, she died childless, ending the poet's hopes of establishing a dynastic family line. (Detail from a painting owned by her parents, Susanna and John Hall.)

4.
THE MERRIE MEETING

The year is 1662. For almost half a century Shakespeare has been lying in his grave near the altar of Holy Trinity Church. In the Rector's quarters at the church resides a new Vicar. His name is John Ward. An earnest soul, concerning his new town and his new neighbors he feels an intense curiosity. Faithfully he keeps a combined diary-commonplace book. Writing in it almost every day, he jots down not only what happens in his own life, but what he thinks, what he sees, what he hears.

An Oxford graduate, Ward had at least heard the name of Shakespeare, knew that he'd long been a Stratford resident, knew that in the days of Queen Elizabeth and King James he'd been among the most popular dramatists, as well as a best-selling poet. (With, changing tastes the popularity of the plays had dipped rather drastically, while the three volumes of poetry had kept selling right along.) In his church almost every day Ward would be reminded of the poet as he walked past the grave that lay under the floor of the chancel. An even more graphic reminder would have been the wall monument put up by Anne Shakespeare, an elaborately-framed bust of the poet that looked down on the grave from a prominent spot on the nearby church wall. If the minister needed to be told of the high regard Shakespeare had earned in his own time, he could read it in the inscription on the wall monument, which placed him in the company of Socrates and Virgil (a literary convention of the time for praising authors and other eminent personages, but still impressive, no doubt, to a casual browser in the church pausing to gaze at the Shakespeare bust). "Stay, passenger!" further exhorts the inscription, and give a thought to the man "whom envious death hath plast / Within this monument: Shakespeare with whom / Quick nature dide . . ."

A more living link to the poet, as Ward soon learned, was the present mistress of New Place, Shakespeare's granddaughter, Elizabeth Hall, then married to her second husband (her first, Thomas Nash, had died in 1647). With both husbands she had been childless, and at age fifty-six had no further hope for offspring. It was a thought that often gave her pain, for she knew how fervently her grandfather had wished to continue his line. With her it ended.

Her present spouse, Sir John Barnard, baronet, owner of an ancient estate at Abington near Stratford, had been knighted by Charles II. Now in Warwickshire,

Elizabeth was known far and wide as Lady Barnard, a title which would have immensely gratified the commoner son of John Shakespeare, merchant and maker of fancy gloves for the wealthy. Two other Shakespeare relatives were also then alive, the grandsons of his sister Joan, George and Thomas Hart, both still living in the old Henley Street place.

The poet's own daughter, Judith, the Reverend Mr. Ward had barely missed knowing. A month or two before he arrived in town to take up his church duties, she had died, aged seventy-seven. Married to the harum-scarum Thomas Quiney, her life had been hard, especially her last years when she had to suffer the deaths of all three of her children, and the disappearance of her husband. About 1650 he abandoned his family and went off to cast his own sorry lot in London. For a decade, Judith lived all alone in a cramped apartment over the Cage Inn, her thoughts often, it may be, ruefully recalling her father's words of warning about young Quiney.

Soon enough Ward's inquisitive, friendly manner brought him confidants in town, and his wide-ranging diary notes began to include snippets about Shakespeare. Rather strangely, however, none came from Lady Barnard or the Hart brothers, or so, from the wording, it would seem. On December 10, 1662, the new Vicar was officially installed at Holy Trinity. Early the next year in his diary he made this note:

> Shakespeare had but 2 daughters, one whereof Mr. Hall the physitian married, and by her had one daughter, to wit, the Lady Barnard of Abington.

Hardly inside information. His next Shakespeare entry, made probably a few weeks later, had a bit more to it — and it must be kept in mind that there was then nothing in print to which Ward or anyone else could turn for knowledge about the poet's life (the first biography — little more than a generalized sketch, and not too reliable — wouldn't appear for another forty-seven years). Combining "facts" apparently picked up in conversation with several sources, the second entry has led to some confusion among scholars:

> I have heard that Mr. Shakespeare was a natural wit, without any art at all; he frequented the plays all his younger time, but in his elder days lived at Stratford, and supplied the stage with 2 plays every year, and for that had an allowance so large that he spent at the rate of 1000 pounds a year, as I have heard.

That wasn't the first mention on record of Shakespeare's "natural wit, without any art" (spontaneous genius, was meant, without the study and honing usually needed to develop talent). But Ward's comment, interestingly, shows that the idea (of course not true) had already found its way as a received fact among the poet's townsmen. The confusion comes in when the second part of the note — after "Stratford" — is taken as belonging to the first part. The writing of an average of two plays a year, and the earning and spending of large annual sums, of course exaggerated in town report, took place not in the poet's hometown but in London during his active years in the theatre.

Ward's third diary entry betrays the fact that in his rummaging after the poet, at least once he ran into people who'd actually read the plays, a few at least, perhaps had seen some in performance. The minister's own feelings of deficiency at the moment must have been acute:

> Remember to peruse Shakespeare's plays, and be versed in them, that I may not be ignorant in the matter.

Finding the plays in print would have presented no particular difficulty. By then there had been separate publication of a dozen or more, as well as two collected editions. Making good his resolution, Ward got hold of a copy of the second (virtually the same as the first, which had been collected and edited after Shakespeare's death by the two fellow actors mentioned in his will, Hemminges and Condell). Remaining as Vicar of Holy Trinity until his death in 1681, Ward may well have become a local Shakespeare authority, but about that nothing is known.

A regrettable lack in the Ward diary is any reference to his sources, the people he spoke with and who gave him his information. Concerning the previous four entries, that didn't make much difference. For the fifth, ever since discovery and publication of the Ward diaries in 1839, it has made a world of difference. Who in Stratford, what man or woman, when and under what circumstances, was it who told the following to the surely attentive Vicar? All that can be deduced as to the date of the entry is that it was made before mid-1663:

> Shakespear, Drayton, and Ben Jonson had a merrie meeting, and it seems drank too hard, for Shakespeare died of a feavour there contracted.

With that tantalizingly off-hand remark Ward's Shakespeare entries come to an end. In the course of a long career at Holy Trinity church he filled up sixteen more such gossipy notebooks. In none of them can be found anything further on the poet. In none does he tell about ever meeting Shakespeare's granddaughter, Lady Barnard, or his grandnephews, the Hart brothers. Here was his most regrettable oversight, especially concerning Lady Barnard. For another eight years she lived on, a gracious, accessible hostess at New Place, where she spent part of each year, and at her husband's estate in nearby Abington.

In February 1670, at age sixty-three, leaving on record not one word about her grandfather, or about his papers and books, long in her possession, Lady Barnard died.

In 1616 Michael Drayton and Ben Jonson were bigger names than Shakespeare. They were easily the best-known, most admired writers in England, Shakespeare taking rank in third place, with some allowing him no better than fourth or fifth. Jonson indeed, because of his classical flair, his position as court poet and favorite playwright of King James, and by force of personality, held sway over all. Drayton, primarily a poet, also wrote and collaborated on plays. Jonson, primarily a writer of plays and masques, also wrote poetry. Both knew and liked Shakespeare. Each other they didn't like, not much, and they often found themselves in competition.

In London during a period of more than a dozen years before and after the turn of the century, starting about 1597, the three would now and then have run into each other at the various theatres, and at the gathering places favored by writers and actors—the famous Mermaid Tavern, obviously, as well as another tavern less famous but equally favored, the Devil's Inn. The evidence for Jonson's friendship with Shakespeare is strong, that for Drayton's and Shakespeare less so, but adequate. Drayton, in fact, who like Shakespeare was Warwickshire born and bred, during many years spent the summer months at a friend's country estate near Stratford, in the village of Clifford Chambers. From there New Place was distant only a mile or a bit more, a leisurely twenty-minute stroll.

While it is certain that Drayton often visited Stratford to see friends—some of them also friends of Shakespeare—no evidence can be cited that actually puts the two together in a room. The best that can be established along that line is that Drayton was once treated for a fever by Shakespeare's son-in-law, Dr. Hall. At different times Hall also cared for Drayton's hosts during those summer visits to the village of Clifford Chambers, Sir Henry and Lady Rainesford.

In his records Hall notes his treatment of the fevered Drayton, though without date: "Mr. Drayton, an excellent poet, labouring of a Tertian [intermittent fever], was cured by the following: Rx the Emetick infusion one ounce, syrup of Violets a spoonful, mix them. This given, wrought very well both upwards and downwards."

A medicinal syrup made of plain violet petals was by no means unusual in the pharmacology of the day, which had its disposal precious little real medicine of any kind. What may have been the nature of the "Emetick infusion" isn't stated in the translation of Hall's Latin prescription, but it was specified by Hall as "Rx p. joz. sy. violor coch. s. tam ore quam alvo recte purgatus & curatus." Whatever it was precisely, the decoction of syrup and purgative must have given the poor poet quite a rough shaking, "upwards and downwards." None of this yields the true nature of the illness.

Whether Hall made a house call at Clifford Chambers, or Drayton dragged himself aching to Hall's Stratford office, can't be said. The date of the treatment

Fig. 11: Michael Drayton (left) and Ben Jonson (right), rivals of Shakespeare in the theater and as poets. In that day both were as well known and well regarded as he, in some ways even better known. Both were with him at the Mermaid Tavern the night of their "merrie meeting" to celebrate the wedding of Judith, the poet's elder daughter. However, the supposed "feavour" he caught that night was not linked to his death.

Besides being rivals the three much admired each other's writings. Drayton, a year older than Shakespeare, outlived him by fifteen years. Jonson, eight years younger than Shakespeare, outlived him by twenty-one years.

could have been any time between 1602, when Hall set up shop in Stratford, and 1631, when Drayton died.

What opinion Drayton personally held on the merits of Shakespeare's writing must be judged on the strength of four and a half lines he wrote in a composition giving his view of English authors who were active in his own time and before, from Chaucer on. The praise he sounds for Shakespeare is high indeed, yet peculiarly subdued, nothing like what he offers several others such as William Alexander and Drummond of Hawthornden:

> And be it said of thee,
> Shakespeare, thou hadst as smooth a comic vein,
> Fitting the sock, and in thy natural brain
> As strong conception and as clear rage
> As anyone that trafficked with the stage.

"Smooth" and "clear" and "strong" aren't the most glowing terms Drayton could have chosen, and they apply only to Shakespeare's writing for the stage. Overlooked are his three best-selling volumes of poetry. Still, the two were competitors, and in any case it isn't necessary to think a man a great writer to like him and enjoy his company.

Ben Jonson, on the other hand, saw the truth, and saw it as did no one else of his time. In an 80-line dedicatory poem in the first collected edition of Shakespeare's plays he spoke as never one poet spoke of another. "Soul of the age!" he cries in hailing his recently dead friend. "The applause, delight, the wonder of our stage!" he styles him, far outshining all of the day's other writers. Only some of the ancients, he insists — Aeschylus, Sophocles, for instance, but no one else from "insolent Greece or haughty Rome" — deserve even to be mentioned in the same breath as the man from Stratford, who was "not of an age, but for all time!" An intense personal nostalgia pervades Jonson's closing lines as he recalls the vanished magic of so many of Shakespeare's opening nights and performances before royalty:

> Sweet Swan of Avon! what a sight it were
> To see thee in our waters yet appear,
> And make those flights upon the banks of Thames
> That so did take Eliza and our James!
> But stay; I see thee in the hemisphere
> Advanced and made a constellation there!
> Shine forth, thou star of poets . . .

The London stage, he finishes, "since thy flight from hence," has been able to do nothing but droop and mourn, its darkness relieved only by "thy volume's light."

Even more to the point for the present investigation, Jonson greatly admired Shakespeare as a man. Himself a boisterous, bohemian personality, warm-hearted, self-centered, intellectually aggressive, he was drawn to his opposite, a man he described as "indeed honest, and of an open and free nature," whom he loved and honored, he said, as much as anyone, "on this side Idolatry."

True, he was more than a little bothered by Shakespeare's lack of "art," and of classical sense and training, and by his tendency in the rush of composition to make silly mistakes. "Many times," complained Jonson, "he fell into those things could not escape laughter. As when he said in the person of Caesar, one speaking to him, *Caesar thou dost me wrong*, and he replied, *Caesar did never wrong, but with just cause*, and such like, which were ridiculous." Another example he gives is a claim by some characters in *The Winter's Tale* that "they had suffered shipwreck in Bohemia, where there is no sea near by some 100 miles." Both of these mistakes — along with a raft of others, no doubt — were pointed out to their author and were gratefully corrected. "But he redeemed his vices with his virtues," adds Jonson. "There was ever more in him to be praised than to be pardoned."

It could have happened, that "merrie meeting" noted by the Reverend Mr. Ward, whether or not as a result of it Shakespeare caught the "feavour" from which supposedly he died. Concerning Drayton and Jonson, however, there is no actual record of the two socializing, and each did have rather an antipathy toward the other. Still, as fellow toilers in the London theatres, especially where others were present, they probably did now and again share a table at some inn or tavern. The question to be first answered about the rumored encounter of the three is *where* it took place, if it did.

Biographers who tend to accept the meeting as true feel pretty sure of themselves about the location, simply assuming that it was either at the Shakespeare house in Stratford, or at Drayton's summer stopping-place, the Rainesford mansion in Clifford Chambers. The twenty-minute walk that separated the two houses made either one possible, and inviting as the site in question. A 1903 book describing the Shakespeare country of Warwickshire has a chapter entitled "A Walk to Clifford Chambers" which envisions the two poets meeting on the road:

> Let us suppose that Drayton came to pay a visit to the Rainesfords at Clifford Manor House . . . He would have to pass along the roads we now pass along, though the commons were not enclosed and hedges were fewer than at present. On those occasions Drayton would naturally meet his friend William Shakespeare of Stratford-on-Avon, sometimes walking to see him at the house he occupied before he bought New Place, and afterwards at New Place. Shakespeare must also have walked over the Cross o' the Hill to Clifford: and so we see the Poet amid surroundings new to most of us . . .

That, too, is possible, even likely — mutual friends in both places must often have drawn visits by both men, even aside from their deliberately calling on each other. The trouble is that no slightest hint during twenty years places Shakespeare at the Rainesford house in Clifford, none has Drayton ever dropping in at New Place. Further, there is Jonson to be considered. Getting him with his slow-moving bulk to that 'merrie meeting' in Warwickshire at either place is no easy task. An arch-Londoner, not given to travel, he almost never left the capital, and again, no record puts him anywhere near Stratford (except once, a fact which has its own peculiar relevance, but which must wait its turn to be considered).

If there really was such a meeting of the three men, and if it didn't take place in Stratford or Clifford, then *where*? Obviously of course in London, where both Drayton and Jonson daily pursued their busy, not to say hectic careers, and to which Shakespeare in his retirement sometimes journeyed on business or just for an outing. Neither Drayton nor Shakespeare was known as much of a drinker — Jonson definitely was — but that needn't mean that they never imbibed a bit too much. Inevitably that brings the trail around to the door of the one place in London known to every writer, actor, and propman, famous for its sumptuous fish dinners and pure canary wine, and where the garrulous Jonson with glass perpetually in hand held court: the Mermaid Tavern in Bread Street.

One of the habitues of that immensely popular watering-place, playwright Francis Beaumont, recalling the many wonderful evenings he'd spent there in company with his theatrical friends, put it this way:

> What things have we seen
> Done at the Mermaid! heard words that have been
> So nimble, and so full of subtle flame,
> As if that every one, from whence they came,
> Had meant to put his whole wit in a jest . . .

Very often those nimble words and thoughts of flame were sparked (so an early tradition says) by the exchanges between Jonson and Shakespeare, each quite in character — Jonson the ready if blustering scholar, Shakespeare the agile improviser. This description of the scene, written when there were people still alive who'd known both men, found the one perfect way to express it:

> Many were the wit-combats betwixt him and Ben Jonson, which two I behold like a Spanish great galleon, and an English man-o-war . . . Jonson was built far higher in learning, solid but slow in his performances. Shakespeare was the English ship, lesser in bulk but lighter in sailing, could turn with all tides, tack about, and take advantage of all winds by the quickness of his wit and invention . . .

At the Mermaid Tavern in London, then, it can with justice be suggested, occurred the famous "merrie meeting."

But when? Is it at all possible to fix or suggest a date for the meeting, even approximately? It is, given certain facts and probabilities, and if the Reverend Mr. Ward's note recording a belief then current in Stratford may be given *some* credence, rather than discarded whole.

The Ward jotting includes four elements: 1) there was a convivial meeting of the three poets; 2) Shakespeare drank somewhat more than usual; 3) he contracted an illness, which caused a fever; 4) as a result of the illness, unnamed and not so much as hinted at, he died. Now while the first three elements, on the available evidence, *may* be true, the fourth, again on the evidence, certainly is *not*.

Neither Jonson nor Drayton, for one thing, ever told of being present when his friend took his fatal illness, though both wrote and talked of him afterward. Jonson, less than three years after Shakespeare's passing, found himself in a situation where he might have put the facts on record — where he might easily have been *expected* to do so — yet didn't. It was in December 1618, and he had made one of his rare moves out of London, trekking north to visit Scotland. While there he stayed for two weeks at Hawthornden, the home of the poet William Drummond. Every day the two talked incessantly, mostly about literature, with the emphasis falling on contemporary authors and their works. Drummond, mightily impressed to have England's leading writer in his home, made copious notes of what was said by his willing guest. In them Shakespeare is twice mentioned. Yet there is nothing about his recent death, no regrets expressed about the loss to literature, nothing said about Jonson's being present when the fatal fever was caught.

Surely Jonson would have known of it if their night on the town had led to his friend's untimely end. Surely in his two weeks' non-stop conversation with his fascinated host at Hawthornden the subject of Shakespeare's recent mournful end would have come up, if Jonson had really been a part of it.

For some minds that glaring omission — taken with the total absence of evidence otherwise — is enough to establish, not that there had been no such meeting, but that, given a meeting, it had not led to Shakespeare's death.

The fourth item in Ward's jotting thus is cancelled. That leaves the other three as the basis for determining the date of the meeting. It's just enough.

Together the picture they provide is clear: as a result of a night of at least mild carousing, a fever of some kind was contracted by the poet. While it didn't cause his death, it did occur *near in time* to that regretted outcome. Was there some particular occasion in the months and weeks preceding his death for which he might have been feted by his two friends? (It's possible, of course, that others were present besides Jonson and Drayton.) One such occasion promptly suggests itself: the marriage of his younger daughter on February 10, 1616. Between mid-February, then, and March 25th, the day he signed his will at New Place, when for whatever reason Shakespeare had gone down to London, there occurred the much-talked-of nocturnal outing, the Reverend Mr. Ward's "merrie meeting." Celebrating the marriage of the thirty-one-year-old Judith, his friends took him to the Mermaid in Bread Street. A regular party with song and drink and many other friends present, it may have been.

The weather at that season was still cold, so the party perhaps was seated at a table near a goodly fire. Steady drinking and smoking, with voluminous talk and frequent eruptions of laughter, in an overheated room heavy with clouds of tobacco smoke — then the bracing chill of the night air on the walk across town to his house in Blackfriars, a long trudge through windy streets and open squares. When he awoke next morning was he disappointed and disgusted to feel his throat raspy, his eyes heavy, his forehead hot?

For a couple or three days, it may be, his aches and pains and fever kept him in bed in London. Then, somewhat recovered, he bundled himself up and went home to Stratford where he knew that loving hands were waiting to tend him.

When you're not feeling well there's no place like your own bed in your own house and the sound of familiar voices.

Not by any means out of the question are rather precise dates for all this, if the basic period of mid-February to late March first be conceded. It is a stray piece of information about the Mermaid and its artistic clientele that does the trick.

In the very year that Shakespeare died, another Mermaid regular — Thomas Coryat, a well-known author and friend of royalty — in a letter happened to mention that the Mermaid "Club" of writers and actors was accustomed to meet "on the first Friday of every month." For the Shakespeare meeting, if it applies, that would mean the first Friday of March, which in 1616 fell on the 6th. Say that his cold and fever kept him in bed for two or three days before he felt able to stand the journey home. If so, he left London on Monday, March 9, or perhaps the next day. Suppose it was the 9th. In that case his arrival home at New Place was on the evening of Wednesday the 10th, or even a day later still if he departed London late on the 9th and made the usual night's stopover at Oxford.

Two weeks later in the study at New Place came his sudden, hurried signing of the heavily corrected will (in place of a standard fair-copy version which would have taken barely an hour to prepare). The shaky script of the last name of the signature — Shakespeare — supplies evidence of some unknown physical impairment or collapse in the hand that wrote it.

For the poet, all unknowingly, that pathetically frantic act was, in sad reality, the beginning of the end.

The evidence is all in. Every clue, every least fact that may be adduced concerning the puzzling death of the world's foremost author has been fairly laid out and discussed. As scattered bits and pieces strewn through many sources, familiar or obscure, those facts and clues have long been available. Will they prove sufficient when fitted together in proper sequence and setting according to their intrinsic quality and value to solve the riddle?

As did our opening chapter, we begin with the poet's arrival home from his visit to London in April 1615 on his fifty-second birthday.

5.
TREMOR CORDIS

I have *tremor cordis* on me;
my heart dances;
But not for joy, not joy . . .
Winter's Tale

For the young and ambitious, London was a fine place to be, full of excitement and interesting people. No one knew that better than Shakespeare. But he'd had enough. Now he looked for a quieter, more even-tenored existence away from minds in a constant glow of scripts and acting and stagecraft. No place for that like his own study in his own house in his own home town, surrounded by family and friends.

Only one thing threatened to mar the picture, that nasty episode of two years before over Susanna. Echoes of it could still be heard in town, and it galled him almost beyond bearing. His first child, Susanna had been the apple of his eye from birth, an affection that grew as she grew, revealing intelligence and a graceful imagination. It was undoubtedly of Susanna he was thinking when in *The Winter's Tale* he paid a tribute to

> . . . the prettiest low-born lass that ever
> Ran on the green-sward. Nothing she does or seems
> But smacks of something greater than herself,
> Too noble for this place . . .

That Susanna was much like her mother — both of them, it seems, strikingly attractive presences — is surely reflected in these few lines from *Pericles*:

> My dearest wife was like this maid, and such a one
> My daughter might have been. My queen's square brows,
> Her stature to an inch, as wand-like straight,
> As silver-voiced, her eyes as jewel-like
> And cased as richly, in pace another Juno.

The thought that his loved daughter, now herself a wife and mother, had been the target of such slanderous foul gossip dragged him down terribly. Even more, he was discouraged by his inability to track down the story's ultimate origin, past the man who'd made it a public scandal, or even to understand what its purpose might have been. Was it merely malicious or had there been a reason behind the lie? Susanna, when asked, said she had no idea what could have set John Lane off like that. Ralph Smith she knew, but only as one of the many Stratfordians she was acquainted with.

The bad thing was the way the story became a silent, nagging presence, the way his nerves would jump to hear anyone use the phrase "runninge of the raynes." That Susanna might have contracted an infection was the furthest thing from possibility, and in the family it was never mentioned. Once he did come close to asking Dr. Hall what he thought — it was from Susanna that he most wanted male heirs — but he didn't.

Not so easy to judge are his feelings for his younger daughter. Certainly he loved and wanted to protect Judith, every bit as much as he loved and wanted to protect the older girl, and did his best to see that she was happy. Being a twin and losing her brother when she was only a little girl, he knew, had placed on her an unusual emotional burden. For some reason she had never learned to write (she made her signature with a mark), and probably couldn't read much, either. No less than with Susanna, though, the poet looked for Judith to continue his line. It was natural he'd worry some when she was slow to choose a husband from what must have been a goodly crowd of suitors.

But eager as he was to see her married, her settling on the town playboy was a crushing disappointment. Everybody knew she could have done much better, might have had any of a dozen upright sons of the town's better-off "gentlemen." Young Quiney, though, was the one she wanted, and she waited patiently till he came round.

At least that finally settled the question — and none too soon, since she'd shortly be looking at her thirty-second birthday. She and Tom were talking of a wedding early in the next year, so maybe there'd be another grandchild by that Christmas. Maybe it'd be a boy!

All during his fifty-second year, more often than he liked, Shakespeare found himself brooding over the agreement he'd signed with the Enclosers. There was nothing actually wrong, nothing illegal about protecting his own interests like that, of course, promising to keep out of the fight if his losses were covered. Enclosure might easily cut in half his annual yield from his lands and the tithes, and it could be a lot worse than that, depending. It had taken him thirty years to get where he was. If he lost it now, all or in large part, at his age he'd never be able to start over again.

Stopping the enclosure movement in Warwickshire was out of the question. Of that he felt convinced. Not with all the Combes' money and influence behind it, and the wily Mainwaring having access to the Lord Chamberlain's ear up in London. Let the town do its best trying to rally the area's more powerful interests to fight the enclosers — true, a few of the wealthiest had already joined them — in the end they'd find that they had only wasted their time and their resources. As it had in so many other places around the country, enclosure was coming to Stratford. Maybe that was good, maybe it was bad. But it was coming.

The hard part for Shakespeare, the distasteful part, had been swinging Tom Greene over, even if it hadn't taken much swinging. As soon as the Combes explained things to Greene, he saw how it was, how he'd be facing his own ruin if he didn't go along. Adding the town clerk's name to the same paper he himself had signed with Replingham didn't really suit the poet, preferring to have it done separately. But the lawyer had pressed him hard, offering a flood of double-talk. Afterward, he realized his mistake in letting his name be linked in a legal document with an official who'd already signed a different contract with the town, pledging to give his best efforts in fighting enclosure.

From January 1615, after his name was written into the Replingham note, Greene didn't do much fighting. Afterward he pretty much left it to others (that, quite definitely, is what the documents say, despite strenuous modern attempts to exonerate the clerk).

That's when the poet's respect for his cousin hit bottom, ending a slide that began several years before when it became clear that Greene's heart was more in business than in literature, the reason Shakespeare had taken him in to start with. It had worsened when Greene stubbornly refused to help in the effort to uncover the true motives of John Lane in starting that terrible rumor about Susanna.

Greene's link to Lane was a close one — his brother was married to Lane's sister — and Shakespeare had expected that he would talk to Lane, find out what was really going on. But he wouldn't. Said his brother had told him to stay out of it, mind his own business, not come around upsetting his wife, Lane's sister.

Greene *knew* something, of that Shakespeare was convinced. Something about Lane and his motives. He was silent because he was protecting someone. That disturbing conclusion, coupled with the sorry way Greene had so blithely turned his coat, letting down the people he'd sworn to protect, finished the clerk with Shakespeare. After that he took pains to avoid the man.

About the enclosure movement, however, though nobody could have predicted it, he proved to be dead wrong. First in late February came a cease and desist order from the court, an injunction that halted everything. Then in April came the final decision by the high bench actually prohibiting enclosure for good. The affected land, directed the court, must be put back just the way it had been before the rumpus started.

While he, along with most of the town, was rather shocked at the outcome, in a way Shakespeare was glad of it. All could now go on just as it had prior to the trouble. His own investment was safe, the town revenues were intact, the common lands would go on yielding crops for Stratford families as they had for centuries, and the hundreds of town poor would not go hungry. Just as important, that private agreement he'd made with the Enclosers could now be scrapped and, he hoped, forgotten.

Outside of the little group immediately involved, no one had known of the agreement. Now it need never be known. The document could be destroyed — his copy, the Replingham copy, and Greene's — leaving no trace of itself.

But perhaps not yet . . . not just yet.

After their final defeat in April 1615, the Combes had again turned ugly. Through the summer months there'd been rumors about them, how they ranted over the court's decision, loudly vowing to keep up the fight. That's all it was, thought many, frustrated rant, and even if they did try again they'd surely get nowhere. The decision against them had been handed down by the Chief Justice himself, Sir Edward Coke. Not even Mainwaring's patron, the Lord Chancellor, could get to a man like Coke.

Still, the rumors kept coming. By summer's end it was being whispered that the Combes, bypassing the regular Warwickshire Assizes, were readying an all-out assault on the London courts. This time it sounded vaguely, uncomfortably possible, and in that case the prudent thing would be to wait. For another six or so months, say until March of next year, 1616, he would retain the documents intact. Meantime he'd pass the word to Replingham and Greene about keeping their copies under lock and key.

In time, he had no doubt, the Combes' threat to enclose Stratford's ancient fields would fade completely away. When he was sure that it had, he'd collect all three copies of the agreement and personally burn them.

Taking notes, lawyer Francis Collins sat at a table in the study at New Place, opposite the poet and his wife. It was late January, 1616. Remaining before Judith's wedding were barely two weeks. Urged by Anne, the poet was finally revising his will.

The week before, he'd talked things over with the prospective bridegroom, Tom Quiney, and it was understood that there would be an immediate marriage settlement on Judith of one hundred pounds outright, and that at least three hundred pounds additional would be specified to the couple in his will. In return Tom was expected to bring to the match one hundred pounds of his own.

Some few other additions and changes in the will were also specified. His wearing apparel — no inconsiderable gift then — he'd leave to his nephews, Joan's three sons — they'd grow into them. Another sum he set aside to be invested for the benefit of his eight-year-old granddaughter Bess Hall. With his wife's ready consent, the household plate, all of it, would become Judith's whether she and her husband still lived at New Place or had moved elsewhere. It *should* be Judith's, insisted Anne. Susanna now had her own set. As for herself, added Anne, just leave her out. If she found herself alone, surviving him, then she'd just go on living with Susanna and wouldn't care about plate or dower rights or anything else. Except the bed! Their old bed she'd like to own herself, in her own name. Put *that* in the will somewhere, she directed with emphasis, and you can forget all the rest!

As was always intended, the great bulk of the estate went to Susanna and her John: besides a large cash bequest, all the scattered properties including New Place, the investments along with the shares in the London acting company, "and all my barnes stables orchardes gardens lands tenementes & hereditaments whatsoever" in Warwickshire and elsewhere, all entailed on Susanna's male heirs to the seventh generation. Susanna and John would keep the estate together, they'd see that it grew, passing it on intact to some male descendant. How satisfying, even thrilling, to think that a hundred, two hundred years from now his descendants would be living lives of elegant accomplishment and privilege at the top of the heap, all because of him!

As he rose to leave, Collins said he'd have a fair copy of the will ready in a week or so. The start of the year was always his busy season for wills, with people suddenly waking up to how time was passing them by.

On February 10th, Judith's wedding went off beautifully. Filling Holy Trinity church was a huge crowd, invited and otherwise (everything the Shakespeares did in public drew a mob of the curious). In her elaborately flowing white gown, the bride was transported to the church in an open, four-horse carriage, to be smilingly welcomed to the altar by the Reverend John Rogers, the same man who'd signed as a witness to the Replingham agreement. After the ceremony a reception was held, no doubt at Quiney's own establishment, the Cage Inn.

For a couple of weeks the newlyweds went away by themselves, then they came back to New Place, where they were to live. Now for Will and Anne the many rooms of the big house wouldn't seem so bare and empty. Susanna and her husband had lived there too for a while at first, but half a dozen years before they'd moved out to their own place around the corner. At last with another young family on the premises there'd be some sounds of life besides the master and his wife.

With the Quineys' return, about the last week of February, Mr. and Mrs. Shakespeare departed for separate visits elsewhere, wisely letting the young couple have the place to themselves for a bit. Anne was making a long-delayed visit to her sisters at Shottery. Shakespeare was off for London on business. Both would be back in a week. Meantime there were the servants to help get the young-sters settled in. That's how Judith preferred it, and her mother understood. More like moving into their own house.

To Collins the poet sent word that he needn't hurry about the fair copy of the will. He was going down to London and would be back early in March. He'd sign it then.

As she'd promised, Anne was back in a week. Her husband, however didn't show up for another five days, arriving on the 10th, weak and bleary-eyed from the remnants of the cold he'd caught the night of that "merrie meeting" in Lon-don. With him was John Robinson, the tenant of the house in Blackfriars where he'd stayed. To Anne he explained that he'd had a night out at the Mermaid with Ben Jonson and some of the others, Michael Drayton and a few from the Globe, to celebrate Judith's wedding. Will Johnson, proprietor of the Mermaid and an old friend, had arranged it, turning one of the regular Friday night get-togethers into a big party.

(Unmentioned was something else of interest arising that jolly Mermaid night — at least it very probably did. Ben Jonson, it seems, revealed that he'd be-gun collecting his plays for publication in a book, to be entitled his "Works." The announcement brought smiles all around. Styling playscripts *Works* had never been done before, and who'd want to buy a whole book of plays anyway? You didn't read plays, you went to see and hear them. To appreciate plays you needed a stage and actors. A few people might buy a book of plays for professional use, writ-ers and actors and such, but how many could that be? Wouldn't people laugh to hear theatrical ephemera dignified as literature? Then Jonson surprised everyone by announcing that he'd already found a publisher. Shakespeare and Drayton, he suggested, should get busy and do the same, and old Heminges agreed, especially about Shakespeare's things. Telling Anne about it later, the poet began to wonder just how many plays he had by now. He'd never stopped to count.)

Unwisely, he confessed, after the party he'd walked all the way to Blackfri-ars in the night air. Caught a bad chill and lay in bed feeling miserable for three days. At last, a good deal recovered, he'd decided to head home. Mr. Robinson had insisted on coming with him, just in case he was needed, and it's true he still felt woozy. Robinson had relatives in the area, so he'd be staying over for a while as a guest at New Place.

Glad to be home, he looked forward to a good long rest. But there was to be no rest. The most harrowing two weeks of Shakespeare's life were at hand. The trouble started next morning with a stunning revelation by his newly married daughter.

Before that part of the story is told, however, one further fact — an obscure fact, up to now neglected — about the Shakespeare family medical history must be entered on the record.

While it is true that in the days of Elizabeth and James mortality rates were higher than they are now (in general, but especially among the young), the Shakespeare family was marked by more frequent and earlier deaths than was usual even for the time. Two of his four sisters perished as infants, and a third was gone at the age of eight. Two of his three brothers also succumbed relatively early, dying at thirty-eight and twenty-seven, and the third lived to only forty-seven. His own son died before he reached twelve, and his three grandsons did little better, dying at twenty-one, nineteen, and six months. He had four nieces and nephews, of whom one, a girl, died at the age of five, and another, a boy, at ten. The descendants of his sister, Joan Hart, sustained several early deaths, and the picture might be made still more harrowing if the poet's parents' families could be traced, his many uncles and aunts.

While no record survives of serious illness touching either of his daughters, his granddaughter, Elizabeth Hall, Susanna's only child, in her late teens suffered much with ill health. At different times she was the victim of chronic facial and neck paralysis with convulsions (torticollis, wryneck), inflammation of the eyes, and a stubborn "Erratick Feavour" producing hot and cold sweats. Treated by her father with elaborate herb-and-spice mixtures and oil rubs, she recovered, though perhaps not for good. "She was delivered from Death and deadly diseases," happily wrote her father in his notes of the case, "and was well, for many years."

In the poet's bloodline *something* was awry.

During the absence of the elder Shakespeares from Stratford, the newlyweds, Mr. and Mrs. Quiney, had received an unpleasant surprise. For committing a serious offense against church law they had been cited to the Ecclesiastical Court. In a prohibited season they had married without asking for or getting the needed dispensation from the Worcester bishop's office. The Rector at Holy Trinity, the Reverend Mr. Rogers, a clergyman of known liberal bent, had no right to perform a wedding at that time without the special license required by church ordinance. The first summons from the court the disgusted Tom had stubbornly ignored, failing to appear, a serious infraction. Promptly served with a second summons, he'd foolishly done the same thing, throwing it aside unanswered.

On the morning of March 11th a nervous Judith came to her father at New Place and told him the disturbing news. Next day, she said, the Ecclesiastical Court would pronounce its sentence on her and her husband. Almost certainly it

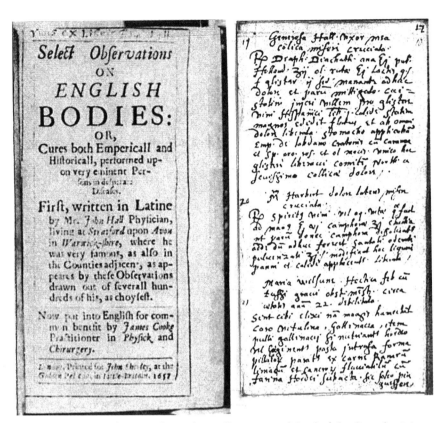

Fig. 12: Shakespeare's son-in-law, John Hall, was one of the day's leading physicians, and he certainly attended his father-in-law at the end, so it is strange that he left no record of the fact. His notebook ("case book") detailing his treatment of many "eminent persons," has no mention of Shakespeare. Some twenty years after Hall's death the book was published as a medical text and was many times reprinted. Above are the book's title page, dated 1657, and, a sheet from Hall's original manuscript written in Latin.

would involve excommunication for both (a harsh penalty, since church membership in England then had far-reaching social as well as religious effects).

Asking what happened, Shakespeare listened as a tearful Judith explained how Tom had taken care of everything. She hadn't known about the need for a special license. She'd left it all to Tom. Called to the room, the wary look on the young man's face showed that he knew very well why he was wanted. No, he replied defensively, he didn't know how the mistake had happened. Vicar Rogers hadn't said anything about a license.

Was that the truth? Was there some other reason why he'd failed to get the church's permission?

No other reason (said with perhaps just a touch of hesitation). Why should there be another reason?

Next morning in the Worcester Cathedral the Bishop's Court declared, among several other rulings, that Mr. and Mrs. Thomas Quiney of Stratford, for their willful failure to comply with church law in the matter of prohibited seasons, were henceforth excommunicate.

It was only some five days later that an even worse blow fell on the now somber atmosphere at New Place. Another summons arrived for Tom, this one issued by the Stratford Ecclesiastical Court and carrying a much more serious charge than that at Worcester: having illicit sexual relations with a local woman, Margaret Wheeler, with pregnancy, and death, resulting. In giving birth — on March 12th, the same day that the Quineys were excommunicated by the Worcester Court — the woman had died, her infant soon following. On the 15th, coinciding with arrival at New Place of the excommunication order, mother and baby were buried in Holy Trinity Churchyard.

Quiney was ordered to stand before the Stratford Court on the morning of March 26th. It would convene as usual in Holy Trinity Church, with proceedings open to the public.

This time in talking with his agitated father-in-law the shamefaced Quiney didn't deny the charge. Before she died, Margaret Wheeler had named him to her parents as the father, had even told some of her friends, and the Shakespeares had simply failed to pick up the floating rumors. At least, they agreed, the Wheeler situation explained why Quiney was in such a hurry to get married, why he hadn't taken time to get the necessary license at Worcester. He was afraid he might be denied, and then people would hear, and the damning story would reach New Place and he'd lose Judith.

If only they'd known! thought Shakespeare. But would it have made any difference? Would Judith have listened to them if they said, poor girl, you know that we *warned* you about him . . .

Still, there was always a way of managing these things if you knew the right people. Tom Greene, wily Tom, he'd know where to begin if anyone did . . . in fact . . . his brother Richard was one of the Bawdy Court Apparitors . . . Richard Greene an Apparitor . . . could, it possibly have been *him* who cited Quiney? . . . could it? . . .

The possibility that one of the Greene brothers, Shakespeare's own cousins, might have been responsible for alerting the court to his son-in-law's guilt greatly disturbed the poet, the bare idea of such a thing finally generating a burst of anger. At his desk he picked up a quill and scribbled a few words on a piece of paper demanding that Tom Greene come immediately to New Place. By messenger the note was sent to the Greene home down at the river.

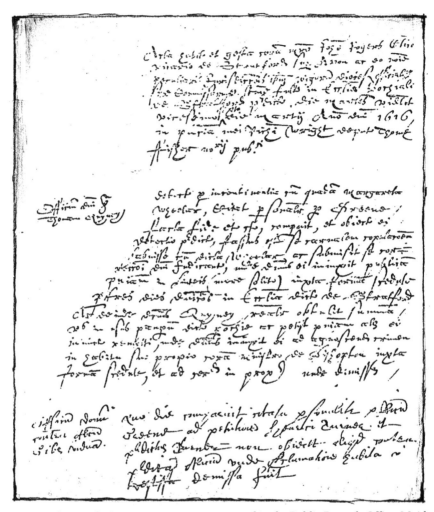

Fig. 13: The Bawdy Court minutes, now preserved in the Public Records Office, Maidstone, Kent (the thirteen-line paragraph at the center). Strangely, though written in 1616, the year of the poet's death, they were entered in a volume covering cases of 1590 to 1608, and were not discovered until the twentieth century.

That summons on its way, he promptly wrote and sent another note, this one to Francis Collins. Please delay drawing up the fair copy of my will, it instructed; there are a few more changes to be made in the bequests, which may prove of some length and complexity. So would Collins please come round?

It was March 20th when Collins finally jangled the bell-pull at New Place. In the study Shakespeare told him that he wanted to change the part of his will referring to Judith. Everything, so far as feasible where a husband was concerned, was to be put beyond Quiney's reach, yet without hurting the girl. For the next hour or so Shakespeare discussed with the lawyer what he wanted, Collins sorting out the legal tangle and deciding how the altered items should be worded. At last Collins said that the first page must be entirely rewritten, and probably, by the time they'd finished, all three pages would be affected.

The changes touching Judith and her husband were thorough.

A hundred and fifty pounds would go to Judith *after* Quiney had furnished a matching sum (fifty of it only after Judith had by legal instrument surrendered her share of the cottage in Chapel Lane — Quiney wasn't going to get his hands on *that* expensive bit of property). The second half of the original three hundred pounds would be payable only three years after his death, and then the whole must be invested for Judith's benefit, not paid out to her. If in that time she had died (here the worried father was probably thinking of the perils of childbirth, then always a risk), the money would go not to her husband, but would be split between his granddaughter, Bess Hall, and his sister, Joan Hart.

Still not satisfied, he instructed Collins to take from the Quineys all the expensive household plate given to them in the earlier will. If Quiney ever got hold of that enticing little item — all those silver and gold platters — the odds were he wouldn't be long selling off the whole collection! When Anne heard about the plate, she insisted that the big silver bowl with the gold trim stay with Judith, the one she'd always liked so much.

Collins gathered up his papers and his notes of the new arrangements. He'd have a fair copy drawn up, he said which would be ready for signing.in a few days. He'd bring it round himself that week or the next.

Tom Greene didn't show up promptly, as Shakespeare's note had demanded. It was four or five days later that he made an appearance at New Place, say March 25th. For the rest of his life he would profoundly regret what happened that afternoon. But it wasn't his fault, he'd insist earnestly, how could he, how could anyone predict the ugly mood that had taken hold of his friend? Could he be expected to know that the poet, always so pleasant, so gentle, so well-mannered, would lose control the way he did? Who knew that he was capable of such anger?

The scene that follows, picturing a rancorous clash between the poet and his cousin, rests on no clear or specific documentary evidence. It is given as the conclusion of one investigator, this author, after long and careful pondering, after much poring over the collateral evidence. But to that warning this claim may be confidently added: that no other passage in or portion of this volume enjoys a more certain reality. For one thing, it is quite evident that the agitated Shakespeare would have demanded — not asked or politely requested — that Greene make use of his considerable influence in town on behalf of the beleaguered Quiney. *Block the action against my son-in-law!* he'd have ordered emphatically. Even surer, as the episode relentlessly unfolds and resolves itself, is the strong probability that Greene would have refused, that he could have done nothing else.

Carrying the process to its unavoidable conclusion, it was from that refusal — Greene's abandoning his relative and long-time benefactor — that there flowed the whole tragic denouement.

The actual details of what happened at that meeting between the overwrought Shakespeare and Greene of course remain unknown, as do the actual words exchanged by the two. But what very probably happened, what was very probably said, are things not hard to picture, as well as the setting and sequence of the scene. In the reconstruction that follows the action is allowed to run without interruption.

Entering the study where Shakespeare stood waiting for him, Greene saw immediately that there was trouble ahead. No handshake, no invitation to sit down, only a curt question almost spat between the grim lips. Did your brother report my son-in-law to the court?

Not really surprised by the question, Greene for a moment kept silent. Then he realized that the truth would come out in the trial record. Yes, he did. It was his duty to do so. Once he was informed, it was his duty.

Duty! That ridiculous Bawdy Court, pushing its nose into everybody's private affairs! What about duty to family? To friends? Was it his duty to disgrace my son-in-law?

Will, you're not thinking —

Tom, this is the second time you've shown up in a family crisis of mine. The *second* time. On the other side . . .

What? . . .

I still say you're not telling me all you know about that despicable cur John Lane and his trashy lies about Susanna.

But Will, I've told you —

Never mind what you told me. What I want from you now is to hear how you're going to help Tom Quiney. Get the thing postponed from tomorrow's session. Then we can find a way to have it dropped altogether. You can do it through your brother, you and him together. You owe me that much . . .

Will, you don't understand —

You're the man who manages things around here for the Council. You know everyone in town. Don't tell me you can't get a postponement. Get it!

Honestly, Will, I can't —

His voice growing strident, with eyes suddenly ablaze, Shakespeare came back: You mean you won't! Won't even try. Why not? Were *you* behind it? Were you? How did your brother find out so fast about Tom and that girl? From you?

No, no, Will, not me. The story was all over town —

It *was* you, wasn't it! You and that ambitious brother of yours. Neither of you gives a damn for anyone else!

The ordinarily gentle-mannered poet was now thoroughly worked up. Threateningly he took a step toward his guest. Backing away, Greene said pleadingly, Take it easy, Will, take it easy. I'm telling you I don't know how it got to Richard —

Did you and Lane together cook up that lie about Susanna and Smith? Now you and your brother set out to get Tom Quiney? What's going on? After all the years you spent living here with us like part of the family!

Another threatening step forward. Again Greene backs off.

It's no use, Will, no use. I'm going. It's no use talking any more, not while you're like this. I'm going.

Turning, Greene walks toward the study door.

Come back here!

Without responding, Greene keeps on toward the closed door. Just as he reaches it he hears a step behind him, then feels hands roughly grab his shoulders. He is spun violently around and before he can react, Shakespeare's hands are at his throat: By God, I want that thing postponed, or I'll . . .

As the strong hands tighten, Greene tries to push his assailant off, but can't. In desperation he throws himself against his attacker. There is a brief struggle, ending with both men falling heavily to the floor, sprawling in a tangle on the thick rug, Shakespeare on top. For a moment Greene lies still, gathering his strength for one forceful shove to free himself.

Suddenly Shakespeare's frantic grip on his throat slackens. In another second the poet goes limp. Then he collapses, his whole weight coming down on Greene, a moment later rolling off to the floor. In a heap he lies on his side, arms and legs bent grotesquely, eyes shut, face contorted.

Bruised and shaken, Greene struggles o his feet. In the doorway appears a maid who'd heard the noise, staring in shocked surprise at her master lying in a bizarre sprawl of twisted limbs on his study floor.

Call for help, mumbles Greene to the maid as he kneels and turns the poet over on his back.

Moments later two male servants hurry in. Carefully they pick up their master, carry him across the room, and stretch him on a couch, placing a pillow under his head.

Eyes still shut, long hair at the sides of his head bunched and disheveled on the pillow, his cheeks ashen, he lies unmoving. In the subdued light of the study the high, rounded forehead and the top of the balding head shine a ghostly white.

Anne rushes in, voluminous skirts flying. Quick, she says to a servant after a glance at her husband, run for Dr. Hall. Tell him that Master Shakespeare has taken very ill. At home. He's to come immediately.

Kneeling on the floor beside the couch, she takes the poet's hand in hers, chafing it gently.

Will? Can you hear me? Will?

Trembling, the heavy eyelids slowly lift and unfocussed eyes stare at Anne's troubled face. When he speaks the voice is a throaty whisper, the words badly shaped.

Anne . . . I can't . . . move . . .

John's coming, Will. Just rest.

Only my right arm a little . . . just the right arm . . . and the leg a little . . . not the left . . .

Anne controls her shock. Just rest, Will. You'll be all right. John will be here in a moment . . .

The heavy eyelids come down. After a few seconds he speaks again, eyes still closed, in his voice a note of sudden excitement: Anne! . . . Anne! Send for Collins. Tell him to bring the will. Get him here now with the will! No delay, Anne . . . now! Get him for me, Anne! Get him! Get the will!

6.
SERGEANT DEATH

Had I but time — as this fell sergeant, Death,
Is strict in his arrest — O, I could tell you —
Hamlet

For exactly thirty days after the poet's collapse, Dr. Hall labored diligently to save his father-in-law, not quite understanding that all his knowledge and all his medicines were powerless to cure paralysis or restore slurred speech. Why the paralysis was partial, only one side losing motion, must have sorely puzzled him. No doubt he'd read about the condition, but would have seen it or something like it only a few times. There were, he knew, a dozen different diagnoses and as many suggested treatments.

Though hampered (unknowingly) by the medical ignorance of the day, but aware of the circumstances that led to the collapse, fully versed in the Shakespeare family medical history, Hall might well have been able to guess at the truth: an apoplectic seizure (sudden blockage of one or more blood vessels in the brain). As a general concept, apoplexy was not unknown to Elizabethan medicine, though little was understood of its actual cause. William Harvey's discovery of the circulation of the blood had not yet been published, so the idea of "stroke" had yet to be formulated. The idea that blood in some manner actually flowed through the body *was* known at the time, a plain fact that is nicely demonstrated by Shakespeare's own reference in *Julius Caesar* to "the ruddy drops that visit my sad heart."

The records of Shakespeare's case and its treatment that were undoubtedly kept by Hall — he kept meticulous accounts of all his patients and their progress — have disappeared. Still it is possible to gain a good idea of what the poet's treatment was like, what medicines were used to what effect. Some years after Hall's death nearly two hundred cases out of the thousands he'd handled during a thirty-year practice were published from his own manuscript as a medical textbook. While none of his patients seems to have sustained an actual stroke, identified and described as such, a few had ailments which in a way resembled it, in externals at least.

Shakespeare had been dead only a few years when Hall treated a young man suffering from what might have been epilepsy, might have been a form of hysteria, and with abdominal complications, "also Hypochondriack Melancholy, with a depravation of both sense and motion of the two middle fingers of the right hand." His first prescription included four ingredients, two of them decipherable as ground flower petals of the borage plant, and *castoreum*, oil from the sex glands of a beaver. This supposedly cured the paralyzed fingers. Then Hall performed a venesection, drawing eight ounces of blood from "the Cephalick vein" (neck or head). At the same time he had the patient swallow some pills of succinic acid, derived from plant stems, followed by a decoction combining half a dozen different flowers, herbs, and spices, including a good dose of nutmeg, and more *castoreum*. Then came sneezing powder, and a bit of *opiat*. "By these means, through the mercy of God," noted Hall with satisfaction, "he was in a short time cured."

Another man, this one sixty years old, who found himself chronically "oppressed with Melancholy, and a Feaver with extraordinary heat, very sleepy, so that he had no sense of his sickness," was completely cured in two weeks. More than twenty separate ingredients went into his first prescription (leaves of mallows, beets, violets, mercury, hops, wormwood, caraway, fennel, etc.). Attached to the soles of the feet was a poultice of sliced radishes in vinegar and salt. Finally an enema was given and leeches applied. "Bidding farewell to Physick . . . he lived many days."

Hall's prescriptions were not so different from those of his colleagues — though in treating scurvy he was among the leaders. One typical example using very disparate materials, called for "prepared Pearl, prepared Coral, burnt Hartshorn, prepared Granats [probably seed of passion flower], each gr. viii, fragments of Jacynt, Smerdines, and Rubies, each gr. iii one leaf of leaf-gold; mix them and make a powder." A certain ingredient in another prescription also is not untypical: "Peacock dung dried, in white wine."

But Hall as a physician must be judged in the difficult context of that medically primitive era. One scholar who studied all his published cases, comparing them with the original manuscript, was impressed: "He appears a dedicated medical man, independent, conscientious, and unbiased, who . . . showed an intuitive understanding of the psychological needs of his patients." Another prominent physician of the time who knew Hall well, said that "he practiced Physik many years and was in great fame for his skill far and near."

Skilled as he was, though, he could not save his father-in-law. For that outcome, however, he must not in any way be blamed, and not only because of the time's defective knowledge and limited pharmacopeia.

What follows, descriptions of three other meetings the poet from his sickbed had with friends, have also been extrapolated from the facts supplied in the foregoing pages. Given what it is known *did* happen, these meetings would have been inevitable, necessarily a part of the story, the logic of the story. The first two — a brief one with his old friend Hamnet Sadler, a longer one with his theatrical colleagues from London — perhaps need the least argument to support them. The third, with lawyer Francis Collins, in its way is equally obvious. However, since more depends on it, directly, concerning the poet's death, it may seem to require stronger proofs. In that case: concede the accuracy in general of the story as developed up through the fight with Greene, then the Collins meeting must have been as pictured here, or nearly so.

First the meeting with Sadler.

Eyes dulled and face drawn, propped up on pillows in his big canopied bed at New Place — of course the famous "second-best bed" — sat the stricken poet. Earnestly he gazed round at the familiar faces gathered on either side of him. Clustered around, standing or sitting, were nine people: Anne, Susanna with her little daughter, Tom and Judith Quiney (five months pregnant with her third child), and his sister Joan Hart with her three teenage sons. Joan's husband William, had died shortly before. Dr. Hall was away tending a patient.

The date is March 28th. Three days have passed since Shakespeare's trembling hand traced his name on the separate sheets of his rough will — his neighbor Shaw and his houseguest Robinson hastily summoned as witnesses. Two days have passed since Tom Quiney received his sentence from a stern church court, public penance to be performed on three successive Sundays. Only two days off is the first degrading performance, when Quiney will be required, while wrapped in a white sheet, to stand on exhibit before the entire Holy Trinity congregation during the whole of a lengthy service. The memory of Quiney's three days of utter disgrace, it is expected, will take a permanent place in the people's memory as a warning to the town's hot-bloods.

At the door sounds a knock. Anne calls Come in, the door swings open and in walks Sadler. On his face is a broad smile.

It's all right, Will, he announces happily, approaching the bed, nothing to worry about, it's all right. Reynolds and he have talked things over quietly with the right people, those in charge. They'd been very understanding about it. Tom's punishment is cancelled, the worst part of it.

The worst part?

He has to pay a fine, then has to admit his guilt to the minister. Not here in Stratford. Over in that sleepy little Bishopton. Not in church. In private in the minister's house. Just the two of them. No white sheet to be worn, just his ordinary clothes. It's settled, Will, and you can rest easy. Nothing to worry about.

From his bed the poet reaches out to take Sadler's hand, thanking him heartily. At the same time he makes a mental note that he'd have to add the names of Sadler and Reynolds to his will. From Anne and the others standing round come similar expressions of gratitude, especially Tom—who from then on ran his inn and kept out of trouble.

Through the long days of early April, stretched flat or sitting up, he remained in bed as the mental sluggishness that had fallen on him like a cloud the day of his collapse began to lift a little. Easing the long daylight hours were the visitors who now began arriving, every day a few, friends and neighbors, and all were taken up to the bedroom for short sessions with the ailing poet. The news of his setback had also reached London, bringing down to Stratford some of his closer theatrical colleagues to lend encouragement. Together about mid-April John Heminges and Richard Burbage arrived, paying a visit that was to yield large consequences for world literature. Neither man left any record of such a visit, but no one can say that it didn't happen, and there are many who will agree that it certainly *did*. Among their topics of conversation, surely, would have been the fact of Ben Jonson's collected *Works*, set to appear in London bookstores in a couple of months.

It was to be a big book, the two would perhaps have explained. In folio form. About eight hundred pages, no less! With a handsome binding, and gold lettering on the cover and spine. In the face of such exciting news—it *was* exciting, opening up another window, another market, for playwrights, bumping them up a notch in the literary scale—the question would have been inevitable: Wouldn't Shakespeare consider doing the same?

Back in London everybody was saying that he really should do it. They'd mentioned the idea to a lot of the actors and writers and all had agreed with the idea. All had said that *his* things deserved book publication easily as much as, maybe even more than, Jonson's.

For Shakespeare, understandably, the idea was still hard to believe. After all these years a real market for a *collection* of printed plays? Enough of a market so a publisher wouldn't lose his shirt? A book with *only* plays in it? Jonson's volume was to have nine of his plays, but also many of his poems and masques—and he was still laughed at for his presumption.

Pressing the idea, Heminges assured the poet that he wouldn't have to do a thing himself. He and Condell would do all the work. They'd gather the manuscripts, pull it all together, do the editing, find a publisher. When it was ready he could look it over, have the final say. All his things in one big volume.

By now, with Shakespeare facing the very real possibility of death, or at least severe disability, it may have been easier to convince him to take the daring step. Fearing that his writing days might be over, he may have acknowledged that it was time to sum up his decades of authorship, to preserve plays that he knew—he *must* have known—possessed a truly unique quality. Whatever the

Fig. 14: Stratford, in Shakespeare's day considered hardly more than a small town, enjoyed a church of magnificent proportions and elegant decoration. His grave is under the chancel floor to the left. It was his position as lay-rector of the church that gave him the privilege of such in-church burial before the high altar, not his literary reputation.

answer he gave to his friends that day at New Place, the fact is that Heminges and Condell soon afterward, say within a year of the poet's death, in their spare time began serious work on the book, now called by some, "incomparably the most important work in the English language."[1] With collecting, arranging, and editing the manuscripts, having a picture of the author engraved and inviting laudatory verses from his friends, and counting the very lengthy production process of the time, it was nearly six years before the now famous First Folio appeared.

With the book, selling at the fairly high price of one pound, at last available in the stores, Heminges wrote that he and Condell had done the work "only to keep the memory of so worthy a Friend and Fellow alive, as was our Shakespeare." In the volume's Introduction he expresses the editors' earnest wish that the poet "had lived to have set forth and overseen his own writings," but fate had "ordained otherwise, and he by death departed from that right." If the First Folio had not been published, it is believed, about half of the poet's total output might have been lost.

By the third week of April, weary after being drenched with Dr. Hall's elixirs, and no doubt at least one blood-letting, with several sessions of radishes-to-the-feet, the dispirited poet noticed something: among the steady stream of visitors who climbed the steps to his bedroom, none were from the town Council. Since word of his collapse ran through town, not a single one of the Council's twenty or so members had come to see him. Half of them he knew personally, a few were old friends who'd known his family. All had stayed away.

For some twenty-seven days he'd been bedridden when at last, through lawyer Francis Collins, he discovered the reason for the unusual neglect. Here again — like the encounter with Thomas Greene pictured earlier — it will be simpler and more effective to show what happened by means of a brief narrative. The facts as laid out in the preceding pages are offered in justification of the specific detail, as well as the words spoken. Accept the story as developed so far, then what follows needs no urging — including the contention that after this meeting, held on April 21st, Shakespeare had fewer than forty-eight hours to live.

Called to New Place, Collins was told to remove from the will the name of Richard Tyler. Then he was to insert five new names, those of Sadler, Reynolds, Heminges, Burbage, and Condell, each to get money for a memorial ring. At this Collins again mentioned the need to rewrite the will in a fair copy, and Shakespeare agreed: the paper he'd signed in such a hurry the month before when he thought he might be dying, he said, did look pretty awful!

Then he went on, in his voice a note of quiet uncertainty.

Tell me, Francis, what are the folks in town saying about all this? I suppose at the Council Hall they've heard about my little scrap with Greene, and the rest?

Yes, of course they've heard. All very surprised and of course they're very sorry and hope you'll be well soon . . .

That's nice to know. My old friends *do* care after all . . .

Of course they do, Will, of course.

You'd hardly know it.

What?

It's been almost a month, Francis. Nobody from the Council has bothered to drop in here. No messages. Nothing.

Yes, well, I . . .

Francis, what's going on? Why am I being ignored?

Going on? What do you mean going on? Nothing's going on, nothing. (Collins' discomfort was plain to see.)

Why haven't I heard something from the Council? I can name a dozen of them who would've been here to see me the day after it happened. What's keeping them away?

Busy. They're very busy.

Try again.

Well, they are . . . with all the . . .

What have they heard about me?

Nothing, Will, nothing!

You know you'll tell me sooner or later. What?

Nothing, nothing . . . just a lot of silly talk.

Tell me.

Ridiculous stuff! Forget it. That stupid enclosure business, That's all. Forget it.

What's the talk?

They're all idiots! Most of them. A few are actually saying that you signed a private agreement with the Combes. Of course I know you didn't and it's only a handful of the Council . . . they say that you promised to keep out of it if your losses are made up. I told you it was nothing.

Who's saying that?

Oh, Foxe and Gibbs and a few of that crowd.

Any evidence?

Forget it, Will . . . they say they've seen a copy of the note. If they have, of course it's a forgery.

Where did they get it?

Who cares, Will! Forget it . . . from one of the Lanes, they say, old Nicholas Lane's grandson. The Combes' lawyer too, that sly creature Replingham . . . Come on, Will, just forget it . . . nobody believes . . .

A sudden weight descended on the sick man's shoulders . . . one of the Lanes . . . of course it *would* be one of them . . . of course! . . . that lying little guttersnipe

John Lane . . . Tom Greene's foul-mouthed relative . . . little bastard!. . . him and Tom both, worthless bastards!

Far into the night the despondent brooding held him in its corrosive grip. When next morning his bleared eyes slowly opened his breathing was labored, his flesh in a tremble. Two days later arrived his fifty-third birthday, April 23rd, and the known day of his death. In the murky darkness of early morning he was suddenly shaken by a violent trembling, followed by partial paralysis. Within minutes the master of New Place — let us agree it was with his loving family gathered around his bed — stopped breathing, the victim of an apoplectic seizure.

In the old Shakespeare house in Henley Street, the room in which the poet was born is still lovingly preserved, sparsely furnished but containing a large Elizabethan bed (not of course the original). Minutes away, in Chapel Street, is the now-vacant site of the much grander house in which he died. If the facts as laid out and interpreted in the preceding pages are accepted as at least probable, then it may with full justice be said that the second event was in large part controlled by the first.

In Shakespeare's physical make-up, as in that of his three brothers, to mention only those, lurked a constitutional weakness inherited at birth. To have it prove fatal only time and a trigger were needed. On what seems good evidence, that weakness is now identified as a congenital circulatory disorder, one liable sooner or later to cause a stroke or some type of coronary distress. The trigger itself, on testimony equally convincing, is identified as a relentless pile-up of emotional tension to the breaking point, arising out of a mounting series of grievous personal and family embarrassments.

Would it have happened without that explosive if brief struggle with Greene in the New Place library? Possibly. Quite possibly. But the very logic of that unfortunate encounter really seems to develop a momentum, an inevitability, of its own. At the very least, Greene's family connection with John Lane would have led the angry Shakespeare to question him about Lane's shocking accusation of Susanna. Only natural would be Shakespeare's expecting Greene to help in running down the rumor to its source and uncovering its purpose. Whether Greene responded positively or not, Shakespeare certainly and justifiably would have suspected him of knowing a good deal more than he let on. Under provocation like that — his loved daughter vilely traduced, his family honor stained--any man might lose control, more so when also goaded by the troubles of his other daughter and her scapegrace husband.

Left hanging at this point is a single loose end, of some peculiar interest if less than major significance. If Shakespeare's death happened suddenly — in some sense not unexpected but still suddenly, as would have been the case with stroke or some form of heart attack — how and when did he convey to his family the now famous quatrain he wrote for his gravestone? It could of course have been written and given to Anne in a casual way at any time before his collapse on March 25th as something he wanted to have done when his time came. More likely it was written as he lay brooding in bed during the month after the fight with Greene, all the time fearing that he might not recover, that death in fact was imminent.

No old sexton in forty or fifty years would dig out what remained of *him* to make room for somebody else! No one would pick up *his* skull as Hamlet had Yorick's and grow witty over it!

He knew his sextons, how superstitious they all were. He knew that those four threatening lines would scare them off for a few hundred years:

> Good frend for Jesus sake forbeare
> To digg the dust encloased heare!.
> Bleste be the man that spares thes stones
> And curst be he that moves my bones.

Short, unadorned, very much to the point. Not impressive as poetry. But not at all bad when taken as the last utterance of a man whose brilliantly exuberant mind had at last been subdued, and whose hand trembled as he wrote the plaintive words.

7
FORBEARE TO DIGG

Today in Holy Trinity Church the space beneath the chancel floor is occupied by seven graves, stretching in a row from wall to wall. The story they tell is a curious, even perhaps a revealing one, indicating Shakespeare's unfailing desire even in death to leave behind him a respected name and distinguished family line.

Not only Shakespeare lies there. Four other members of his family have been similarly honored, and it is probable that, if it could have been arranged, all seven chancel graves would hold Shakespeares. It's as if this grouping of the family before the high altar — a signal honor, of much prestige, available to few — was meant to compensate for, to wipe out, any lingering stain left by the several ugly scandals of that final year. Stratford and its good citizens who had so attentively followed those scandals were supplied with a permanent reminder that the Shakespeares had survived with honor intact, had in fact risen far above the awful pile-up of trials and sufferings.

Burial before the high altar was not accorded Shakespeare because of his literary standing or character. It was his official connection with town government as part owner of the tithes (purchased by him some years before, a form of investment of the time) that made him a lay-rector of Holy Trinity, giving him the right of burial within the church before the high altar. The other members of his family, however, did not share in this right, so the fact that they now lie there beside him points to a special arrangement of some sort. Perhaps it was made by the dying poet himself, to be carried out by surviving family members.

The first grave on the left (an observer's left facing the altar) holds Mrs. Shakespeare, who died in 1623 after surviving her husband just over seven years. Next to her, the graves almost touching, is the poet (1616), and on his left is his granddaughter's husband, Thomas Nashe (died 1647). Next to Nashe is Dr. Hall, Susanna's husband, who died a dozen years *before* Nashe (1635, which probably means that at Hall's death the present Nashe grave was occupied by someone other than Nashe, a burial too recent to be disturbed). Then comes Susanna Hall, the poet's elder daughter (died 1649). The last two graves (on the observer's right) are occupied by a Mr. and Mrs. Watts (1691 and 1704).

Fig. 15: (top right) Holy Trinity Church in Stratford in which Shakespeare was baptized and is buried, was in existence more than 200 years before the poet's birth.
(Left) Shakespeare's grave under the chancel floor in Holy Trinity Church is marked by the metal floor plaque at middle foreground. Next to him on the left is the grave of his wife Anne. On the wall above the graves is attached his memorial monument holding the famous bust (see iillus. p. 7). Made in London, it was commissioned and approved by his wife and others of his family.

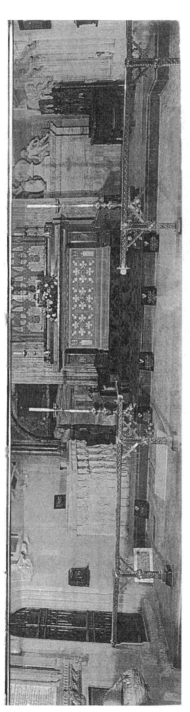

1623	1616	1647	1635	1649	1691	1704
Anne Shakespeare	William Shakespeare	Thomas Nashe	John Hall	Susanna Hall	Watts	Watts
the poet's wife		First husband of the poet's granddaughter	the poet's son-in-law, a physician	the poet's elder daughter, wife of John Hall	no relation to the poet, husband of Mrs. Watts	no relation to the poet, wife of Mr. Watts

Fig. 16: The Chancel Graves, Holy Trinity Church, Stratford.
The five Shakespeare family graves (from the left) correspond to the small floor-plaques in the photo.

It is probable that the two Watts graves had earlier held other occupants, for if they had been empty and available they would almost certainly have received the bodies of Shakespeare's two grandsons (Richard and Thomas Quiney, both died 1639, ages nineteen and twenty-one) or that of his younger daughter Judith Quiney (died 1661, aged 78), or that of his granddaughter, Elizabeth Hall (Mrs. Nashe, later Lady Barnard, died 1670).

Ironically, the fate that Shakespeare was so anxious to avoid for him- self — having his bones removed to the charnel house — did happen to his daugh- ter Susanna, or so it seems. In 1707 a son of the Watts' died. Susanna's grave lay next to that of Mr. Watts, and by then she had been dead for nearly sixty years, so was a candidate for removal.[1] The inscription on her tombstone was erased and replaced by one for young Watts, seeming to indicate that Susanna was in fact re- moved. Only in 1844 — by which time Shakespeare stood alone and triumphant at the head of English literature — was Susanna's epitaph restored to its former place on the gravestone, and that of Watts erased. The body within, though, is still no doubt that of young Watts, not Susanna. ("The scandal of such early and irregular exhumation," states one respected historian, "was a crying grievance throughout England in the seventeenth century.")

Any number of stories have come down about Shakespeare's grave being ac- cidentally broached, and his coffin or his bones being seen. But all are apocryphal, prompted perhaps by the fact that about 1690 repairs were made to the large, flat gravestone, which had become displaced by the settling of the ground under it. The slab was taken up, the ground leveled and firmed, and the stone replaced.

One thing is certain. Since April 25, 1616, no part of what the poet himself called "the dust enclosed here," no inch of the chamber, whether of earth or brick, that holds his coffin, has been seen by mortal eyes.

---

1 By then, 1707, no immediate Shakespeare family member remained to contest the removal. Still living were at least two of the poet's collateral descendants, great-grandnephews. Whether these may have tried to stop Susanna's removal, or could have, is problematic.

APPENDIX A
THE DOCUMENTS

A. SHAKESPEARE'S WILL

Since it is not given here for its antiquarian interest, I have added paragraphing and modernized the spelling. After all, the will is a dry legal document, not meant for breezing through. That very fact has disappointed many a past scholar looking hopefully for touches of the poet. But a lyrical tone in the document's carefully-drawn clauses I personally think would give reason for suspicion. Shakespeare was a professional writer. He used his compositional abilities where appropriate and not otherwise. Surely he'd laugh to hear it said that a will might display the testator's literary skills or creative bent!

For the clearest, most easily read transcription of the original, exactly as drawn and amended, see either the *Riverside Shakespeare*, 1832–34, or Rogers, *Second Best Bed*, 4–9.

According to a later note written on the lower right corner of page three (omitted here), probate was granted on June 22, 1616, to John Hall.

Deletions are shown by a cross-out line. Interlined additions are given in boldface type. Unneded capitals are reduced, and punctuation added.

Vicesimo quinto ~~Januarii~~ Martii Anno Regni domini Nostri Jacobi nunc Regis Anglie etc. decimo quarto & Scotie xlix Annoque domini 1616.

Testamentum: Wm Shackspeare

Recognoscatur: In the name of God amen. I William Shakespeare of Stratford Upon Avon in the county of Warwickshire, gentleman, in perfect health & memory, God be praised, do make and ordain this my last will and testament in manner and form following. That is to say, first I commend my soul into the hands of God my creator, hoping and assuredly believing through the only merits of Jesus Christ my Savior to be made partaker of life everlasting, and my body to the earth whereof it is made.

Item: I give and bequeath unto my ~~sonne in L~~ daughter Judith one hundred and fifty pounds of lawful English money, to be paid unto her in manner and form following: that is to say, one hundred pounds **in discharge of her marriage**

portion within one year after my decease, with consideration after the rate of two shillings in the pound for so long time as the same shall be unpaid unto her after my decease; and the fifty pounds residue thereof upon her surrendering **of** or giving of such sufficient security as the overseers of this my will shall like of to surrender or grant all her estate and right that shall descend or come unto her after my decease or **that she** now hath of in or to one Copyhold tenement with appurtenances lying and being in Stratford Upon Avon aforesaid in the said county of Warwickshire, being parcel or holden of the Manor of Rowington, unto my daughter Susanna Hall and her heirs forever.

Item: I give and bequeath unto my said daughter Judith one hundred and fifty pounds more if she or any issue of her body be living at the end of three years next ensuing the day of the date of this my will, during which time the Executors to pay her consideration, from my decease, according to the rate aforesaid. And if she die within the said term without issue of her body, then my will is & I do give & bequeath one hundred pounds thereof to my niece Elizabeth Hall, and the fifty pounds to be set forth by my Executors during the life of my sister Joan Hart, and the use and profit thereof coming shall be paid to my said sister Joan, and after her decease the said fifty pounds shall remain amongst the children of my said sister, equally to be divided amongst them. But if my said daughter Judith be living at the end of the said three years, or any issue of her body, then my will is & so I devise and bequeath, the said hundred and fifty pounds to be set out **by my executors and overseers** for the best benefit of her & her issue, & **the stock** not **to be** paid unto her so long as she shall be married & Covert Baron ~~by my executors and overseers~~ but my will is that she shall have the consideration yearly paid unto her during her life, and after her decease the said stock and consideration to be paid to her children if she have any, and if not to her executors or assigns, she living the said term after my decease, provided that if such husband as she shall, at the end of the said three years be married unto, or at any time after, do sufficiently assure unto her and the issue of her body, lands answerable to the portion, by this my will given unto her & to be adjudged so by my executors & overseers, then my will is that the said one hundred and fifty pounds shall be paid to such husband as shall make such assurance, to his own use.

Item: I give and bequeath unto my said sister Joan twenty pounds & all my wearing apparel, to be paid and delivered within one year after my decease. And I do will and devise unto her the house with appurtenances in Stratford wherein she dwelleth, for her natural life under the yearly rent of ten shillings. Item: I. give and bequeath unto her three sons William Hart, **blank**[1] Hart, Michael Hart five pounds apiece, to be paid within one year after my decease ~~to be set out for her within one year after my decease by my executors with the advise and direction~~

---

1. Giving directions to lawyer Collins, Shakespeare probably said simply. "My three nephews," expecting Collins to fill in the names, and he at the moment failed to recall that of Thomas.

~~of my overseers for her best profit until her marriage, and then the same with the increase thereof to be paid unto her.~~

Item: I give and bequeath unto her **the said Elizabeth Hall** all my plate **except my broad silver and gilt bowl** that I now have at the date of this my will.

Item: I give and bequeath unto the poor of Stratford aforesaid ten pounds. To Mr. Thomas Combe my sword. To Thomas Russell esquire five pounds. To Francis Collins of the borough of Warwick in the county of Warwickshire, gentleman, thirteen pounds six shillings & eight pence, to be paid within one year after my decease.

Item: I give and bequeath to Mr. ~~Richard Tyler thelder~~ Hamlett Sadler twenty-six shillings eight pence to buy him a ring **to William Reynolds, gentleman, twenty-six shillings eight pence to buy him a ring**, to my godson William Walker twenty shillings in gold. To Anthony Nashe, gentleman, twenty-six shillings eight pence & to John Nashe twenty-six shillings **eight pence** ~~in gold~~ **and to my fellows John Heminges, Richard Burbage, & Henry Condell twenty-six shillings eight pence apiece to buy them rings**.

Item: I give, will, bequeath, and devise unto my daughter Susanna Hall **for better enabling of her to perform this my will & towards the performance thereof** all that Capital, Messuage, or tenement with the appurtenances **in Stratford aforesaid** called the New Place, wherein I now dwell, and two messuages or tenements with appurtenances situate, lying, and being in Henley Street within the borough of Stratford aforesaid, and all my barns, stables, orchards, gardens, lands, tenements & hereditaments whatsoever situate, lying, and being, or to be had, received, perceived, or taken within the towns, hamlets, villages, fields and grounds of Stratford Upon Avon, Old Stratford, Bishopton, & Welcombe, or in any of them in the said county of Warwickshire, and also all that messuage or tenement, with the appurtenances, wherein one John Robinson dwelleth, situate, lying, and being in the Blakfriars, London, near the Wardrobe, and all other my lands, tenements, and hereditaments whatsoever, to have & to hold, all and singular, the said premises with their appurtenances unto the said Susanna Hall for & during the term of her natural life, and after her decease to the first son of her body lawfully issuing, & to the heirs males of the body of the said first son lawfully issuing, and for default of such issue, to the second son of her body lawfully issuing, & so to the heirs males of the body of the said second son lawfully issuing, & for default of such heirs, to the third son of the body of the said Susanna lawfully issuing, & of the heirs males of the body of the said third son lawfully issuing. And for default of such issue the same so to be and remain to the fourth ~~sonne~~, fifth, sixth, and seventh sons of her body lawfully issuing one after another, and to the heirs males of the said fourth, fifth, sixth, and seventh sons lawfully, issuing, in such manner as it is before limited to be & remain to the first, second, and third sons of her body, & to their heirs males. And for default of such issue, the said premises to be & remain to my said niece Hall & the heirs males of her body lawfully issuing, & for default of such issue to my daughter Judith & the heirs males of her body lawfully issuing. And for default of such issue to the right heirs of the said William Shackspere forever

   Item: **I give unto my wife my second best bed with the furniture.**

   Item: I give & bequeath to my said daughter Judith my broad silver gilt bowl. All the rest of my goods, chattels, leases, plate, jewels & household stuff whatsoever, after my debts and legacies paid & my funeral expenses discharged, I give, devise, and bequeath to my son in law John Hall, gentleman, and my daughter Susanna his wife, whom I ordain & make executors of this my last will and testament. And I do entreat and appoint **the said** Thomas Russell, Esquire, & Francis Collins, gentleman, to be overseers hereof. And do revoke all former wills, & publish this to be my last will and testament. In witness whereof I have here-unto put my ~~seal~~ **hand** the day and year first above written.

Witness to the publishing   By me William Shakspeare
hereof: Francis Collins
Julius Shaw
John Robinson
Hamnet Sadler
Robert Whatcott

B. THE ENCLOSURE AGREEMENT

The sole existing document is preserved in the archives of the Shakespeare Birthplace Trust at Stratford. It consists of a single sheet of paper with a five-line heading followed by twenty-one neatly written lines of text, ending with the signatures of four witnesses. It is not the whole original, but a partial copy, certainly made by Thomas Greene. The omitted parts list Shakespeare's specific land holdings in the affected area (Bearman, *Stratford Records*, 54–55).

The two separate references to Greene, in the original, were obviously written in between the lines. In this copy they are inserted as if part of the original text. The damning nature of this agreement, for both Shakespeare and Greene, of course is denied by those scholars who are unable to see the human side of the poet as less than perfect. On what was probably its first publication, in the Halliwell biography of 1848, the sole comment is that it "appears to have been executed in anticipation of the enclosure being made" (268). The most recent treatment of it is different only in phrasing: by signing the document Shakespeare "might play a neutral role" in the struggle (Honan, *A Life*, 387). In between there have been only a few lonely voices willing to face the reality.

Again, for easier reading, spelling is modernized, miscellaneous capitals dropped, and paragraphing added.

Vicesimo octavo die Octobris anno Domini 1614.

Articles of agreement indented [and] made between William Shakespeare of Stratford in the county of Warwickshire, gentleman, on the one party, and William Replingham of Great Harborrow in the county of Warwickshire, gentleman, on the other party, the day and year abovesaid.

Inter alia.[2]

Item: The said William Replingham, for him, his heirs, executors and assigns, doth covenant and agree to and with the said William Shackespeare, his heirs and assigns, that he, the said William Replingham, his heirs or assigns, shall upon reasonable request, satisfy, content, and make recompense unto him, the said William Shackspeare, or his assigns, for all such loss, detriment, and hindrance as he, the said William Shackspeare, his heirs and assigns, and one Thomas Greene, gent., shall or may be thought, in the view and judgment of four indifferent persons, to be indifferently elected by the said William and William, and their heirs, and in default of the said William Replingham, by the said William Shackspeare or his heirs only, to survey and judge the same, to sustain or incur for or in respect of the increasing of the yearly value of the tithes, they the said

---

2. "Among other things." A standard legal phrase, the words are written separately in the left margin. They indicate that a portion of the original has been omitted from this copy.

William Shackspeare and Thomas, do jointly or severally hold and enjoy in the said fields, or any of them, by reason of any enclosure or decay of tillage there meant and intended by the said William Replingham; and that the said William Replingham and his heirs shall procure such sufficient security unto the said William Shackspeare and his heirs, for the performance of these covenants, as shall be devised by learned counsel.

In witness whereof the parties abovesaid, to these presents interchangably their hands and seals have put, the day and year first above written.

Sealed and delivered in the presence of us,

Thomas Lucas	Anthonie Nasshe
John Rogers	Mich Olney

C. THE BAWDY COURT MINUTES

On its discovery in 1964 by Hugh Hanley, Kent County Archivist, Thomas Quiney's Bawdy Court appearance was quickly recognized as having singular importance. Hanley himself suggested its role in causing a revision of Shakespeare's will, and he adds, "The news that the young man had got himself into trouble with another woman and that an illegitimate child was on the way would have come as a blow to Shakespeare's pride" ("Shakespeare's Family"). Brinkworth in his fuller study of the Bawdy Court records carried the thought still further, calling the Quiney-Wheeler affair "The talk of the town . . . the biggest scandal that Stratford had seen for years . . . a terribly searing experience" for the poet (*Bawdy Court*, 80). Brinkworth assumes, however, that Shakespeare by then had already fallen ill, perhaps a victim of the "feavour" mentioned by the Reverend Mr. Ward. He thinks it may have been the shame of the Quiney scandal, mother and baby both dead, that finished him. I see Shakespeare's "illness" as having *resulted* from several crushing blows, of which the Quiney scandal was one.

For whatever reason, the fact that the young woman involved became pregnant, then died with her baby in childbirth, is not mentioned in the Bawdy Court record. But of course the court was well aware of all the circumstances.

In the original there is no explanation of why the Quiney entry of March 26, 1616, is inserted in a record book which ends in 1608. Entries in the book's final 38 pages are continuous (pp. 37–74, covering cases of 1606–1608), except for pp. 66–67. These two pages, which must have been left blank in 1608, contain the minutes of the 1616 Quiney court, including brief notices of three other cases (see Brinkworth, *Bawdy Court*, 143). Page 68 returns to the cases of 1608. Use of the two blank pages for the Quiney record, of course, must have been quite deliberate, the purpose certainly not a matter of routine filing.

Previous commentators assume that Shakespeare would have known of the Wheeler charge long before Quiney's appearance in court. I conclude that he didn't hear of it until a *few days* before the scheduled appearance, say March 23rd or 24th.

The original document is in Latin (see above, p. 64, for a facsimile (from Brinkworth, 79.). As quoted in the Hanley article all contractions in the original are spelled out. The session was held before John Rogers, Vicar of Holy Trinity, and Richard Wright, notary public, on Thursday, 26 March 1616:

OFFICIUM DOMINI CONTRA Thomam Quyney detectum pro incontinentia cum quadam Margareta Wheeler, citatum personaliter per Greene facta fide etc., comparuit, et objecta ei detectio predicta, fessus est se carnalem copulacionem habuisse cum dicta Wheeler, ac submisit se correctioni domini Judicantis, unde dominus ei iniunxit publicam penitenciam in Linteis (more solito) iuxta formam scedule per tres dies dominicos in Ecclesia dicta de Stratford Ac deinde dictus Quyney realiter obtulit summam Vs in usus pauperum dicte parochie ac petiit penitenciam alias ei iniunctam remitti, unde dominus iniunxit ei ad agnoscendum crimen in habitu suo proprio coram ministro de Bishopton iuxta formam scedule, et ad certificandum in proxima unde dimissus.

The English translation given in Brinkworth (*Bawdy Court*, 143) is a condensed paraphrase. Here I follow the fuller, more precise translation provided by Hanley in the *Times Literary Supplement*, filling in a few phrases he omits:

THE OFFICE OF THE JUDGE AGAINST Thomas Quiney. Presented for incontinence with a certain Margaret Wheeler, personally cited by Greene [text missing?] he appeared, and when the said presentment was brought against him, he confessed that he had had carnal intercourse with the said Wheeler, and submitted himself to the correction of the judge. Wherefore the Judge enjoined on him public penance clothed in a sheet (according to custom) . . . for three Sundays in the said church of Stratford. And then the said Quiney offered the sum of five shillings to the use of the poor of the said parish, and requested that the said penance imposed on him should be remitted, wherefor the judge enjoined on him to acknowledge his fault in his own attire before the Minister of Bishopton, and to certify this at the next court. And so he was dismissed.

The phrase, "And then the said Quiney *realiter* offered the sum," is given by Brinkworth as "Thereafter he proffered the sum." This seems to allow for the passage of some time, at least a few days, between pronouncement of the sentence and its reduction. That, I'd say, fits nicely with my suggestion that Shakespeare's friends, Sadler and Reynolds, at his request brought pressure to bear on the court (see above, 71).

It was also Hanley, in his *Times* article, who first reported the death and burial that same March of the otherwise unknown Margaret Wheeler and her infant.

APPENDIX B
IN DEFENSE OF ANNE SHAKESPEARE

Shakespeare's marriage to Anne Hathaway, its nature and stability, whether happy, whether a love match or not, and so on, has been discussed for some time with opinion offered on both sides, though with little information to go on. At present the question has by attrition settled down to its having been a more or less normal marriage. With the appearance in 2004 of a new biographical work by Stephen Greenblatt (*Will in the World: How Shakespeare Became Shakespeare*), however, Anne at last finds herself targeted for permanent, wholesale disgrace. The damage is done not by any new or significant evidence, but solely by way of Greenblatt's own bald assertions interpreting Shakespeare's treatment of love and marriage in the plays.

As a result of his studies, Greenblatt finds in general that the poet had "a strange, ineradicable distaste" for his wife, an aversion which "he felt deep within him." Certain scenes in the plays "seem to draw on a deep pool of bitterness about a miserable marriage." Also detectable is Shakespeare's "unwillingness or inability to imagine a married couple in a relationship of sustained intimacy." In Greenblatt's estimate all this betrays in the playwright "a deep skepticism" about any man's chances for wedded harmony.

Having sketched out what he sees as the likelihood of Shakespeare's marital woes — their nature, depth, and to an extent their effect on his art — Greenblatt then commits the usual error in this type of critical study: he assumes as proved what he has only postulated, magically turning surmise into fact. Quoting a brief passage concerning love and marriage from *Twelfth Night* he ties it to the assumed difficulties in the Shakespeare household. "How could he have written Orsino's words," he asks earnestly, "without in some sense bringing his own life, his disappointment, frustration, and loneliness, to bear upon them?" So Shakespeare's supposed "distaste" for the mother of his children, and his assumed "bitterness" about marriage, have bred three more doleful — and wholly unproved — defects and blemishes in his young life.

(The *Twelfth Night* passage has Duke Orsino advising that a woman marrying should take as husband "an elder than herself," supposedly Shakespeare's oblique reference to Anne being eight years older than he. But the reason he gives is that *men* are apt to be emotionally unstable, so are inclined to lose interest and fervor as wives age. If Shakespeare is here blaming anyone for anything, then it's himself, and for his own inattention. He is *not* complaining of "disappointment, frustration, and loneliness" in his marriage.[3]

Another revealing passage, in Greenblatt's view, turns up in *Love's Labor's Lost*, supplying further indication of the poet's disappointment. Here the play's lover, blithely concludes Greenblatt, "is treated with irony, distaste, and contempt . . . these may be precisely the feelings evoked in Shakespeare when he looked back upon his own marriage." Since composition of the play dates to the early 1590s it seems that poor Anne, while raising his children, and doing a very good job of it, had to suffer her husband's unexplained "contempt" for a full quarter-century before his death delivered her.

The comedies especially, thinks Greenblatt, betray a peculiar absence of true love, for him a quite suggestive oversight. "There is scarcely a single pair of lovers who seem deeply, inwardly suited for one another," all showing "strikingly little long-term promise of mutual understanding." This generalized, not to say sweeping and certainly arguable conclusion (that "scarcely" is dropped much too casually into the mix) the reader is invited to apply willy-nilly to the poet's personal affairs.

Shakespeare's last will and testament, with its famous bequest to Anne of the "second-best bed," also draws Greenblatt's keenly discerning eye. "As he left the world he did not want to think of his wealth going to his wife," he stats flatly, so to Anne "he left nothing, nothing at all," except that embarrassing bed. Dismissing one critic's sensible suggestion that this bequest in reality was a well-understood gesture of love, expressing "a husband's tender remembrances," the annoyed Greenblatt tartly replies, "the notion of tenderness is absurd wishful thinking . . . by specifying a single object [the bed] the testator was in effect attempting to wipe out the widow's customary one-third life interest — that is, to disinherit her." Then, promptly and lamely, he admits to being unsure of all this and calls on "legal historians" to pronounce on the charge. But they already had. Anne's dower interest in her husband's estate was inalienable. It could not be taken away and need not be specified. This is aside from the fact that she had two married daughters who would be caring for her and to whom went the bulk of the estate.[4]

---

3. Another passage supposedly giving a personal memory, often cited, is in *The Tempest* (iv, 1, 15–22). Prospero warns that premarital sex will bring to a marriage "barren hate, sour-eyed disdain, and discord," which as some think is the author's own rueful memory of the results of his own infraction with Anne. But here again context is everything. Prospero is talking as a *father*, to a prospective son-in-law, so is saying the *expected* thing. If such were at all true of the Shakespeares, the poet would never have put it into his play, where it could be read by his wife, his daughters, and a mob of his relatives. He felt safe including it *because* it was known that his marriage was, and had always been, a happy one.

4. See above, p. 15, for a discussion of the will in relation to Anne, and an explanation as to exactly why she is not further mentioned (she *was* mentioned but herself withdrew in favor of her daughter Judith when the will was redrawn).

Greenblatt's real fault in all this extrapolating from the plays is simple excess, a massive, blatant overuse of what we'll call the Probability Factor. That peculiar fault, it is safe to say, offers the single greatest temptation facing the professional Shakespeare scholar, because of the dearth of information coupled with a consuming desire to know more. Greenblatt's offenses in this regard set a new standard of recklessness, so frequent and so loose is his appeal to probability. So deftly, in fact, is each instance of it slipped into place in his text that it easily slides past even an attentive reader's notice.

In building an argument, a certain limited use of the weak links of probability is permissible, helping to bridge gaps that would otherwise halt a promising line of thought in its tracks. But a ridiculously towering heap of them soon becomes self-defeating, a form of parody that turns the argument round on itself.

Greenblatt's chapter on the marriage of Anne and Will covers thirty pages (118–48). Threaded quietly through those thirty pages can be found no fewer than seventy-eight occurrences of the Probability Factor. Short and unobtrusive as they are, only by picking out and listing them is their pernicious presence made palpable. To get the full, curiously crazed effect, all must be noted, given here in their original sequence through those thirty pages:

> If — if — may have been — even if — even if — almost certainly — almost certainly — may have — would have — perhaps — if — if — might conclude — may not — may be — perhaps — might have — perhaps — is likely — might — likely — may have — more likely — may have — seems valid — perhaps — perhaps too — conceivably — unlikely — apparently — must have — seems likely — entirely possible — must have — perhaps — would have been — seems to have — perhaps — seems to — perhaps — may not — seems to hold — virtually — seems — seems — seems — perhaps — perhaps — may have — perhaps — may have — as if — may have — may have — seem to — even if — in all likelihood — possible — if — might be — perhaps — conceivably — might — perhaps — perhaps — if so — evidently — imagine — perhaps — may have — perhaps — perhaps — seems to — may have — probably — perhaps — seems to — may have

A giddily meandering list indeed! What degree of certainty can be extracted from it? At how many removes from reality, from anything in the least resembling fact or truth, can such determined groping be said to stand? Is *any* result of so frail and shabby a process worth lingering over?

One last, unpleasant suggestion ends Greenblatt's chapter on Anne, no longer phrased as probable but put forward as assured and undoubted. "When he thought of the afterlife, the last thing he wanted was to be mingled with the woman he married." That dour conclusion, no whit earned, derives solely from the four-line verse etched on the poet's gravestone invoking a curse on anyone "that moves my bones." Most observers believe that the lines are aimed at those church sextons who regularly removed old burials from interior graves to outside charnel houses to make room for newer interments. "The scandal of such early and irregular exhumation was a crying grievance throughout Enland in the seventeenth century," wrote Sir Sidney Lee, and he quotes from Thomas Browne's *Hydriotaphia* the complaint about "the tragical abomination of being knav'd out of our graves and having our skulls made drinking bowls." But Greenblatt without the least warrant ignores all this and insists that Shakespeare "may have feared still more that one day his grave would be opened to let in the body of Anne Shakespeare." Thus Greenblatt, again gratuitously (note the "may have"), hangs one final slur on the unfortunate woman.

Employing that same handy little privilege of the Probability Factor, but much more reasonably, a quite opposite likelihood can he raised — starting with the probability that it may *not* have been a shotgun wedding, as is too often assumed because of the pregnancy and the age disparity. It may as easily have been a true love match with young Will as the ardent pursuer and Anne perhaps, for obvious reasons, the hesitant if eager one. For thirty-four years the two were together, being parted only by death. During all that time, furthermore — with Will striving to make it in the worlds of literature and the stage, far more difficult then than now — there is no least hint of a falling-out, or rancor, or bad blood between them.

Anne Shakespeare may, in fact, have been the *most* important person in the life and career of her husband, the one with the *most* abiding faith in him and his literary ambitions. Before he got his start, she may well have been the *only* one! The world that loves and honors Will Shakespeare may owe more to his wife, to the woman he loved, than anyone knows or can guess.

I will go one irresistible step further. Flatly I'll declare my firm belief that Shakespeare's greatest, most celebrated and memorable female creation in the plays — Cleopatra in *Antony and Cleopatra* — is modeled largely on his wife, is Anne herself portrayed as she was when the two were first together, happy in their early love, some thirty years before. No greater tribute has ever been paid a woman by her husband. An unprovable assertion at the moment, yes, but not at all unlikely, and what a world of speculation it opens!

In addition, the fact that Anne was a strikingly attractive presence can be read in some of her husband's lines in *Pericles* (written at about the same time as *Antony and Cleopatra*). Looking at and describing a beautiful young woman, Pericles says wonderingly that she is the image of his wife:

> . . . my queen's square brows,
> Her stature to an inch, as wand-like straight,
> As silver-voiced, her eyes as jewel-like
> And cased as richly, in pace another Juno . . .

A statuesque woman, in other words, of regal bearing, naturally graceful, with remarkable eyes, a lovely face, and a voice that caressed the ears: *that*, in her husband's loving estimate, forms the portrait of Anne Shakespeare. Who will be crass enough to say otherwise?

Notes and Sources

As explained in the Prologue, the separate chapters in this book are closely interlocked: Chapters Two, Three, and Four expand on the events pictured in Chapter One, then Chapters Five and Six doubling back on the preceding two. As a result, the same event and incidents come under notice several times. But simple repetition seems preferable to a tangled effort at cross-referencing.

Aside from closely analyzing and discussing all items of evidence, some additional information is offered which readers may find of interest.

Sources are given in shortened form and may be fully identified by a glance at the bibliography. For citing quoted matter, the opening few words of the quote are repeated. Down the left-hand margin are *page* numbers.

PROLOGUE: STRANGE BUSINESS

Since the facts and assertions in the Prologue are meant in a preliminary way and are noticed and cited where they occur later in the text, no sources are given here. My own visits to Stratford and to Holy Trinity Church took place in 1966 and 1993. Photographs of the church's interior, I found, often do not convey a true sense of the building's size and proportions. For what was really, when first built, a small-town, country church it is unexpectedly large and impressive.

CHAPTER ONE: MR. SHAKESPEARE AND FAMILY

3–4   **New Place and its neighbors**: Chambers, *Facts and Problems*; Lee, *A Life*; and Fripp, *Man and Artist*, passim; Eccles, *Warwickshire*, 111–28; Bentley, *Handbook*, 22–69; Adams, *Life*, 440–58; Schoenbaum, *Lives*, 2–29. Too often biographies of Shakespeare make it seem that he existed in splendid isolation. In truth, whether in London or at home, he was part of large and varied groups.

4   **Shakespeare family deaths**: See the genealogical charts in Lee, *A Life*, 514; Wilson, *Evidence*, 453; Honan, *Shakespeare*, 412; Brown, *Shakespeare*, 33. The various deaths are separately discussed in Halliwell-Phillips, *Outlines*;

Adams, *Life*; Norman, *Friend*; Rowse, *Biography*; and Kay, *Life, Works*, passim. The usual comment about the frequency of early death in Elizabethan England hardly applies here.

4   "Grief fills the room" — *King John* III, iv, 93–98.

4–5   **His plans for a family line**: This fond hope, in general, is admitted or mentioned, to a more or less degree, by most biographers, though none dwell on it. Yet it can easily be spotted as the main driving force behind all Shakespeare's personal and business activity in his latter years. His will is perhaps the clearest proof of this, a fact well expressed by one respected biographer:

> Shakespeare's will had one dominant, driving purpose: to leave all the property intact to a single male descendant. John Shakespeare's eldest and only surviving son was determined to fulfill his father's dream of a Shakespeare family established in perpetuity among the landed gentry of Warwickshire, and what sounds like a complicated series of bequests had a single end in view. The land had been bought, the land had been protected, and the land was to go to a male heir. It was true that at present there was no male heir, but Susanna was still a young woman and there was no reason why she might not still have a son. If she did not, her daughter Elizabeth might have a son, and if this failed also, there was Judith. (Chute, *Shakespeare*, 317)

Sadly, the dream was dashed. Susanna bore no more children, Elizabeth though twice married had none at all, and Judith's three sons all died young.

5   **Susanna accused**: Lee, *A Life*, 464; Fripp, *Artist*, 813; Adams, *Life*, 452; Levi, *Life and Times*, 336–37; Gray, *Son-in-Law*, 166–67; Honan, *Life*, 384–85.

6   "about 5 weekes past" — Lee, *A Life*, 464, quoting from the original records in the Worcester Diocesan Registry.

6   **Biographers' neglect**: The reluctance of Shakespeare biographers to do more than mention this unpleasant incident in passing is evident (see for instance Schoenbaum, *Lives*, 27; Rowse, *Biography*, 450; Kay, *His Life*, 395; Ackroyd, *Biography*, 500). A more recent biographer, Honan (*Life*), goes a bit further, suggesting that Lane's motive was a political one, his intention being to harm not Susanna but her husband. Perhaps, but that doesn't go to the charge itself or its effect on the poet and the town and this avoidance of the charge against Susanna has somewhat distorted its effect on Shakespeare. Rafe Smith's father, William Smith, was an alderman in Stratford (Joseph, 50). He lived in Henley Street a few doors down from Shakespeare's New Place, so would

probably have known the Shakespeares as neighbors, as probably would his son Rafe. Dr. Hall treated at least two Smiths of Stratford, a man aged 38 and a woman aged 54 (perhaps Rafe's mother). Joseph, 117, and page 4 in the Hall casebook. Also Hall, *Observations,* 50. No further details given.

6-7 **Susanna's epitaph**: Chambers, *Facts and Problems,* 12, and personal inspection. The complete epitaphs of Anne Shakespeare and Dr. Hall, both, engraved on their tombstones in Latin, are also given in Chambers (9, 11). It is supposed that Susanna's was written by her husband, but no one really knows. Whoever wrote it knew her well and admired and loved her.

7 "letters, patents, deedes," — Chambers, *Facts and Problems,* 160. For some interesting speculation on Shakespeare's purchase of the Blackfriars Gatehouse, linking it to his supposed Catholic sympathies, see Williamson, *Day,* 101–9; also Milward, "Shakespeare and Catholicism." If Shakespeare was indeed a secret Catholic, the fact could have some bearing on his last hours and burial, not as to the cause of death but touching some of the minor attending circumstances. See the Notes to Chapter Six, below.

8-9 **The enclosure campaign in Stratford**: Ingleby, *Enclosure* (1885) is still the fullest over-all treatment, giving maps of the affected area and related correspondence, also a full transcript of Thomas Greene's diary of the affair. It is a complicated subject, though, and there is no up-to-date handling of it. I have also consulted Bearman, *Stratford Records,* 49–59; Chambers, *Facts and Problems,* 141–52; Lee, *A Life,* 331–34; and Bentley, *Handbook,* 51-56. The act of enclosure was another of those societal changes that, generally, worked short-term harm for many and gain for a few, with long-term good for all or most. The real question was whether it could be done while avoiding the worst impact on defenseless commoners, who lost all access to arable land, needed for a family's economic stability.

9 **Shakespeare's private agreement**: Bearman, *Stratford Records,* 52–54; Chambers, *Facts and Problems,* 141–42; Fripp, *Artist,* 806; Adams, *Life,* 455, all of whom give or quote the original document.

9 "reveals a hitherto" — Holden, *Shakespeare,* 315. Here again biographers have tended to avoid drawing what seems really an obvious and inevitable conclusion, that the enclosers by guaranteeing him against loss in effect bought Shakespeare's silence. Among older biographers Adams is rather typical, saying merely that "with characteristic astuteness, Shakespeare deemed it wise to accept this absolute guarantee rather than run the risk of

a serious loss" (*Life*, 455). Among more recent discussions, Rowse tosses off the whole incident by saying that Shakespeare "apparently did not think the enclosure would be proceeded with, but he was protected anyway" (*Biography*, 450). Schoenbaum is more careful, saying that "What view Shakespeare held on the question we do not know," and the private agreement meant that he didn't "get embroiled in the fierce passions that the issue aroused" (*Lives*, 35). Kay (*Life, Work*, 399) thinks it barely possible that Shakespeare "was secretly on Mainwaring's side" (leader of the enclosers), but there he drops the sensitive topic. Honan gives the enclosure matter three whole pages, then concludes only that the Replingham agreement allowed Shakespeare to "play a neutral role in any struggle to come" (*Life*, 387). A 1974 play tries to dramatize the question — *Bingo*, by Edward Bond, which had a brief London run with John Gielgud in the lead — and carries the matter to its limit. Shakespeare is openly accused of siding with the town's moneyed interests against the people, a sin of selfishness for which Bond makes him pay by contritely swallowing poison.

10   **Thomas Quiney's embroilments and the Wheeler pregnancy**: Brinkworth, *Bawdy Court*, 78–81; Eccles, *Warwickshire*, 139–40; Lee, *A Life*, 464–65; Adams, *Life*, 458–63; Levi, *Life and Times*, 338–40; Schoenbaum, *Lives*, 28–29; Honan, *Life*, 391–93; Hanley, "Family." Discussion is reserved for later in text and Notes.

CHAPTER TWO: THE SILVER GILT BOWL

13-16 **Shakespeare's will**: Chambers, *Facts and Problems*, 169–80; Fripp, *Stratford*, 61–30; Halliwell, *Life*, 272–81; Bentley, *Handbook*, 57–63; Eccles, *Warwickshire*, 118–27; Rogers, *Second Best Bed*, 1–19; Hamilton, *In Search*, 61–87. Who it was that first demonstrated how the initial page of the will had been wholly rewritten I have been unable to find. Halliwell (*Life*, 1848) has no mention of it, nor does Lee (*A Life*, 1898). Adams gives a brief description (*Life*, 462), but he has the lawyer Collins actually doing the rewrite at New Place on March 25th while talking with the ailing poet. However, the revisions were certainly ordered by Shakespeare some ten days before that. The clearest early description of the page-one rewrite is in Chambers, *Facts and Problems*, 175. The fact of a rewrite is now generally accepted, no other explanation being able to satisfy the physical evidence.

To date no commentator has ventured to suggest what might have appeared on the old, discarded first page, all assuming that it treated Judith only, as does the fresh page. Postulating, as I do, an extended mention of

Anne Shakespeare on the old page is not at all unreasonable. Nothing that can be stated or guessed at eliminates the possibility — or say the strong probability — of such a mention. Since nearly everything said about Anne in her husband's biographies rests on possibility, this claim too should be given its fair weight.

15 **Richard Tyler**: Eccles, *Warwickshire*, 124–25; Fripp, *Artist*, 872–73. No one has shown much interest in Tyler, or why he was removed from the will. Eccles suggests that the reason was his supposed mishandling of a town fund for the destitute, being "unreasonably slack" in his accounts, a charge Tyler rejected, appealing directly to the Lord Chancellor. It hardly seems sufficient.

15 **The five added names**: That the insertion — between the lines — of Sadler, Reynolds, Heminges, Burbage, and Condell, and the deletion of Tyler, was done some days *after* the signing of the will on March 25th has not before been suggested. Some reason for the action was needed — none has ever been offered aside from its having been an "afterthought" — and for Sadler and Reynolds the one I propose satisfies all conditions. The addition of the other three is explained in Chapter Six.

22–23 **Date of the rewritten page one**: If the will itself was signed on March 25th, which it was, then the extensive alteration of page one was certainly discussed and ordered earlier. Since it was the troubles of Thomas Quiney that precipitated the changes, and since these became known to Shakespeare just prior to mid-March, then a date of March 15th, latest, for Shakespeare's meeting at New Place with Collins to order the changes is most probable, I would say certain.

23 **Court summons of Thomas Quiney**: The license affair — Eccles, *Warwickshire*, 139–40; Fripp, *Artist*, 822–24; Adams, *Life*, 458–59; Honan, *Life*, 391–93. The Wheeler affair — Brinkworth, *Bawdy Court*, 78–80, 143; Hanley (who in 1964 discovered the original Bawdy Court record, reporting and commenting on the find in "Family"). For further discussion see Chapter Five and its Notes.

23 **John Robinson**: Williamson, *Day*, 106–7; Lee, *A Life*, 485; Fripp, *Artist*, 768; Chambers, *Facts and Problems*, 169. That this John Robinson may not have been the London man but a Stratford resident — town records reveal at least one Robinson family — is the claim of some. The possibility cannot be ruled out, yet where there is already one John Robinson in Shakespeare's life

there seems no need to ring in an alternate, about whom nothing is known. One guess is that the Stratford Robinson was a servant in the Shakespeare household at New Place (as also the other unknown witness to the will, Robert Whatcott). Perhaps, but it's *only* a guess, nothing whatever being known about the domestic help at New Place, aside from the obvious need for a large staff. The London Robinson came of a family very active in the Catholic cause. One brother was a Jesuit priest. Both before and after Shakespeare's purchase of the Blackfriars house, tenanted by Robinson, it served as a secret refuge for Catholic priests on the run.

26   **Rough state of the will**: The woefully unfinished condition of the document is admitted by all who do more than glance at it. One modern study, by a lawyer, found it to be thoroughly "mangled," in sober reality "as defective a document as ever went unchallenged in the courts of law and literature," blatantly showing "one defect after another, one oddity after another," all explained only by "suppositions" (Stalker, "Forgery?" 8). Also see Chambers, *Facts and Problems*, 177–78. Hamilton, *In Search*, 63–65, also notes the will's exceeding roughness, but he does so in dogged pursuit of his lonely personal theory that the entire will is in Shakespeare's hand, all too obviously not the case.

27–28 **Analysis of the Shakespeare signatures**: Halliwell, *Life*, 279; Thompson, *Handwriting*, 10–29; Greenwood, *Signatures*, 45–58; Rogers, *Second Best*, 28–29; Hamilton, *In Search*, 66–79; Wilson, *Evidence*, 382–86; Leftwich, *Disease*, 31–40. Greenwood was first to suggest that the poet's page-three signature was not wholly in his own hand, only the surname. Before that it was thought that the obvious deterioration in penmanship of the surname was caused by Shakespeare's assumed "illness" (whatever it was), his hand becoming unsteady as he wrote. But the breakdown in control between the final *m* of William and the *S* of Shakspere is so sudden and complete that two different hands — one healthy, the other weakened by debility — are inescapably called for.

That the signature on pages 1 and 2 of the will were written in early April, some ten days after: the signature on page three, follows logically from my conclusion that the five new signatures were added not at the initial rewrite, but afterwards. If page three was signed by the poet on March 25th, as is generally believed, and page two was signed in early April, as I suggest, then it may be concluded that the page one signature was also written in early April, at the same time as page one. If not, if it was done on March 25th along with the signature on page three, then page two would have been left unattested, which no lawyer then or now would have allowed.

24 "carnal copulation" — Brinkworth, *Bawdy Court*, 143. The same record refers to the act as "incontinence," which today has taken on other meanings beyond sexual activity.

25 **The Bawdy Court minutes**: Brinkworth, *Bawdy Court*, 5, 117, 142–43. Strangely, the fact of the misplaced Quiney entry is not highlighted by Brinkworth, nor is any explanation offered. The entering of that record on a blank page of the 1608 court entries, however, eight years out of sequence, was consciously done, and the only plausible reason is an effort to hide it from public view, then and later. For the present location of the whole minutes see Brinkworth, *Bawdy Court*, 117; Schoenbaum, *Lives*, 204; and Wilson, *Evidence*, 388, 449. When and how they reached the Kent office archives no one knows. They now form part of the Sackville collection.

27 **The different inks**: Rogers, *Second Best Bed*, 18; Thompson, *Handwriting*, 167.

28 **Hurried signing of the will**: Several observers have thought that the official signing of the will on March 25th would have been a more or less hasty affair, perhaps connected with some unknown illness of the poet, perhaps the "feavour" mentioned by the Reverend Mr. Ward. In 1916 a leading palaeographer, Sir Edward Maunde Thompson, suggested that because of the traditional fever, "the condition of the patient became so critical that the draft will had to be used without waiting for a fair engrossment . . . there can be no question that at the date of the will he was sorely stricken; of this the imperfections in the handwriting of the signatures affords ample evidence," in fact indicates that he was "a dying man" (*Shakespeare's Handwriting*, 11, 13). In 1926 Thompson, not satisfied with a simple fever, went a hesitant step further: "the seizure must have been very unexpected and alarming, and rather suggests that something more critical than the traditional fever had fastened on the stricken man." With discovery of the Bawdy Court minutes forty years later, Brinkworth concluded that the Quiney-Wheeler scandal was the "something more critical" that had crushed the already ill poet: "May it not have been the sudden knowledge that the court had decided after all to insist on the appearance of Thomas Quiney in the full publicity of the parish church to answer for his dastardly conduct? It came as the awful culmination of the disgrace which had been hanging over the family for weeks. It would have been a bad blow for a father-in-law in full health. To a very sick man it may well have proved fatal" (*Bawdy Court*, 83). In this book I carry the Thompson-Brinkworth thesis to what I see as its logical, indeed inevitable conclusion, adding several other shocks suffered by the poet about the same time, and drawing a fuller, more detailed picture of the

developing tragedy than has yet been attempted. Unexpectedly I find that the present book is the first whole book to offer a reasoned, document-based solution to the problem of the poet's death, surprising in a field overflowing with book-length Shakespeare studies of all sorts. I am not quite sure what explains the odd oversight, the topic being so intrinsically compelling: the world's greatest writer dying of unknown causes at an age which should have found him in the fullness of his powers.

CHAPTER THREE: THE REPLINGHAM NOTE

29   **Mrs. Shakespeare in biography**: Somewhat puzzling to me is the way this good woman has tended to be slighted in accounts of her husband's life and career. In the total absence of any direct evidence about her personally — none has ever turned up — indirect evidence should count all the more. For one thing, there is the testimony of her two daughters, the fact that she was much loved by them. The epitaph on her gravestone, beside that of her husband, bears a six-line Latin verse inscription expressing their deep love and admiration for her, actually classing her with the resurrected Jesus. In return for the precious gift of life she gave them,

> Mother, alas! I give thee but a stone.
> O! might some angel blest remove its weight,
> Thy form should issue like thy Savior's own . . .

Add the fact of the Shakespeare's three-decade-plus marriage, Anne's patient stewardship of New Place with her husband gone so often, her burial beside him, and the absence of anything negative in the marriage, and I think she may be allowed to have earned a more sympathetic and important share in her husband's life and career than is now accorded her.[1]

30   **Anne's Stratford relatives and neighbors**: Eccles, *Warwickshire*; Fripp, *Stratford*, Chambers, *Facts and Problems*, all passim. Also Bentley, *Handbook*, 22–69; Schoenbaum, *Lives*, 25–29; Rowse, *Biography*, 56–58; and for the Hathaway family: Lee, *A Life*, 505–17; Eccles, *Warwickshire*, 63–73; Adams, *Life*, 65–76; Honan, *Life*, 231–33.

30–31 **Thomas Greene**: Halliday, *Companion*, 248; Ingleby, *Enclosure*, i–xiii; Lee, *A Life*, 476; Eccles, *Warwickshire*, 131–39; Adams, *Life*, 422; Chambers, *Facts and Problems*, 149–52; Kay, *His Life*, 377–78. Greene is one of those shadowy background figures to be met in the lives of most literary greats, always

1. For more on Anne see Appendix B.

there yet seldom seen closely. I am confident that, bringing him to center stage as I do, here and in Chapter Five, I have to an extent restored a figure of hitherto unguessed importance in the poet's life, and not only at its end. That Shakespeare took an interest in his development as a poet, bringing him into his house as a veritable protégé, is only an educated guess, the evidence being scant. But Greene did write poetry, in quality at least competent, as the few surviving examples show. This sonnet in praise of Michael Drayton appeared in a 1603 volume of Drayton's poems:

> What Ornament might I devise to fit
> Th'aspiring height of thy admired spirit?
> Or what fair garland worthy is to sit
> On thy blest brows, that compass in all merit?
> Thou shalt not crownèd be with common bays,
> Because for thee it is a crown too low;
> Apollo's tree can yield thee simple praise —
> It is too dull a vesture for thy brow;
> But with a wreath of stars shalt thou be crowned,
> Which, when thy working temples do sustain,
> Will like the spheres be ever moving round
> After the royal music of thy brain:
> Thy skill doth equal Phoebus', not thy birth;
> He to Heaven gives music, thou to earth.
> (quoted from Fripp, *Stratford*, 59)

A longer and more ambitious effort was his welcoming ode in celebration of King James' accession to the throne in 1603: *A Poet's Vision and A Prince's Glory* (Newdigate, *Drayton*, 200). Though he seems not to have published much, other examples of his writing may have survived, but no one to date has felt interested enough in him to expend the considerable research effort that would be required. Still, if my surmise is correct, that Shakespeare was impressed enough by his poetic potential to try and help him, further study along this line may well turn up important lost information on Shakespeare in a new role, that of literary adviser or sponsor. Nor has anyone commented on the highly relevant and surely fascinating fact that Greene with his family made his home with the Shakespeare's at New Place while the poet was writing at the very height of his powers (perhaps *Hamlet*, but certainly *Othello*, *Lear*, and *Macbeth*), yet left no least word of reminiscence, despite outliving the poet by twenty years. In his own last years, it is known, Greene went to London where he was connected with the courts. No detail of his life there, or anywhere after he left Stratford, is now available. In any case, whether as protégé or not, Greene with his family did live for many years at New Place with the Shakespeare family, an arrangement for which no reason was offered, then or since. Even his supposed relation to the poet is problematic. The claim that he was a cousin comes from Greene himself, in an incidental note (Ingleby, *Enclosure*, 4, 37) where he refers to Shakespeare as "my cosen", but no one has convincingly shown by what links the relationship existed. The fact of Greene's absence from Shakespeare's will seems not to have been before noticed, at least has not been appreciated.

32   **Shakespeare's enclosure agreement**: Bearman, *Records*, 52–56; Chambers, *Facts and Problems*, 141–42; also see above, notes for pp. 8–9.

33   "deceived and dealt evilly" — Eccles, *Warwickshire*, 127–29. The comment was never officially rescinded.

33   **Greene's written contract with the Council**: Ingleby, *Enclosure*, ix-xii. Though favoring Greene, Ingleby admits he acted "like an elector selling his vote to the highest bidder."

33   "at my cosen Shakespeare" — Ingleby, *Enclosure*, iii, (Diary), 1; also Chambers, *Facts and Problems*, 142.

35   "Against Whitehall Wall" — Ingleby, *Enclosure*, (Diary), 1.

35   "Letters written one to" — Ingleby, *Enclosure*, iii; also Chambers, *Facts and Problems*, 143.

35   "wherein live above seven" — Ingleby, *Enclosure*, 16. The letter was sent out by Greene, but was presented as from Stratford's "Bayliffe and Burgesses."

35   **Secrecy of the Replingham Note**: The evidence for this is mostly of the negative sort: taking secrecy as a working hypothesis, I searched for anything *against* it, but found nothing at all, not the least hint. Not well understood is the fact that the existing document is a partial copy made by Greene himself (see above, 33). The originals have disappeared.

37–38 **Greene's "diary"**: consists of four leaves written on both sides, comprising 120 entries dated 15 Nov. 1614 to 19 Feb. 1616. It was discovered and published in stages, 1814 to 1863. The only complete printing now available is in Ingleby, *Enclosure*.

37   "Sept Mr Shakespeare's" — Ingleby, *Enclosure*, 23. Bearman, *Records*, 58.

38 "after many promises" — Ingleby, *Enclosure*, 24.

39 **Replingham's visit to Greene**: Ingleby, *Enclosure*, 7; also Chambers, *Facts and Problems*, 143. The entry, dated Jan. 11, 1615, reads: "At night Mr. Replingham supped with me and Mr Barnes . . . he assured me before Mr Barnes that I should be well dealt withall, confessing former promises by himself and Mr Manneryng [Mainwaring] & his agreement for me with my cosen Shakespeare." The question arises, *why* Greene recorded things that put him in a bad light. He may for some unclear reason have thought he was protecting himself, and in any case he probably never intended the record to be seen by others. How it was that the four separate leaves of his "diary" turned up two hundred years later in the town archives can only be guessed.

42 **Greene and John Lane**: Fripp, *Artist*, 841–44; Lee, *A Life*, 473–75; Chambers, *Facts and Problems*, 12, 122; Adams, *Life*, 52–55. Not quite brothers-in-law, in a small place like Stratford they were certainly well known to each other.

42 "running of the raynes" — Lee, *A Life*, 464, quoting from the original record (Worcester Diocesan Registry, Act Book No. 9). Also Gray, *Son-in-law*, 166–67, 207–8, and Halliwell-Phillipps, *Outlines*, 243–44. The reference by Dr. Hall is in his *Observations*, where it occurs twice, in the Table of Contents, first under G ("Gonorrhea, see Running of the Reins"), and then under R ("Running of the Reins"). "Reins" was a general term meaning the loins, thus applicable to various organs in that location (familiar also from the Coverdale Psalter). It is used by Falstaff in *Merry Wives of Windsor*, V.3.23.

42 **The Apparitor Richard Greene**: No particular notice has been taken of the fact that in the Greene family of Warwick there were three boys, not two, Thomas, John, and Richard, as well as a girl, Margaret. The fact itself is mentioned only by Chambers (*Facts and Problems*, 150), and then only in passing. Like Thomas and John, the Apparitor Greene was also a Stratford town official (Brinkworth, *Bawdy Court*, 22, where it is also noted that Richard Greene acted for the Bawdy Court from February 1607 to March 1616, when he reported and summoned Thomas Quiney in the Wheeler affair). If this Richard Greene was not in fact the brother of Thomas and John — a remote possibility in the present fragmentary state of the records — then he was certainly a cousin, which for my purposes comes to the same thing.

The access enjoyed by all three Greenes to the various town and church records makes it likely that it was one or all of them who managed to bury the minutes of the Quiney-Wheeler case by inserting them in the wrong ledger (see Chapter Two). That this deft manipulation was done to appease the enraged Shakespeare (see Chapter Five), or after his death to mollify Anne and the Quineys, I take to be certain.

CHAPTER FOUR: MERRIE MEETING

45   **The Reverend Mr. Ward**: The diary, more accurately a commonplace hook, covers some twenty years, 1661–1682, and comprises seventeen small volumes. They were unknown in Shakespeare circles until their 1839 publication, edited by C. Severn. The four mentions of Shakespeare here quoted are his only references to the poet. As to who among his flock may have told Ward the story of the Jonson-Drayton meeting, there is not the least clue. Such an unfavorable tale certainly would not have come from Lady Barnard or the Hart brothers. The brevity of the Ward jotting, to my mind, indicates that he was given more detail, which he failed to put down, something about time and place, for instance. His skipping comment on Shakespeare's supposed drinking bout may show that he was more interested in knowing that his townsman counted the famous duo, Jonson and Drayton, among his cronies. When Ward made his notes, Shakespeare's reputation outside of Stratford was still in the doldrums.

46   "Shakespeare had but" — Severn, *Diary*, 182; also in Chambers, *Facts and Problems*, 249.

46   "I have heard that Mr." — Severn, *Diary*, 183; also in Chambers, *Facts and Problems*, 249.

47   "Remember to peruse" — Severn, *Diary*, 184; also in Chambers, *Facts and Problems*, 250. The urgency of this note to himself seems prompted by his finding that Stratfordians *expected* their vicar to be knowledgeable about the hometown poet.

47   "Shakespeare, Drayton, and" — Severn, *Diary*, 183; also in Chambers, *Facts and Problems*, 250.

48   **Jonson and Drayton backgrounds**: Miles, *Ben Jonson*; Riggs, *Ben Jonson*; Kay, *Jonson*, Newdigate, *Drayton*; Elton, *Family and Friends*, all passim.

48 "Mr. Drayton, an excellent" — Hall, *Observations*, 18 (reprint); also 55–56 of the editorial comment.

51 "Let us suppose that — Brassington, *Homeland*, 96–97.

52 "What things have we" — Miles, *Ben Johnson*, 136.

52 "Many were the wit-combats" — Adams, *Life*, 242, quoting from Fuller's *Worthies of England* (1662). Some have, quite unnecessarily, doubted these Mermaid encounters (see Schoenbaum, *Lives*, 94, 294–96). The Mermaid's host, William Johnson, Shakespeare knew well (Bentley, *Handbook*, 23, 84–85).

53 **Jonson and Drummond**: The notes made by Drummond, generally referred to as *The Conversations*, are extensive and have been several times published, the most reliable edition being that edited by Patterson (*Conversations*, 1923). The two brief mentions of Shakespeare comment on his supposed want of art, and his mistake about the shipwreck in Bohemia. If that "merrie meeting" of Jonson, Drayton (also well known to Drummond), and Shakespeare really did produce the illness that took the poet's life, only two and a half years before, how could Jonson have failed to allude to the fact, especially since Shakespeare's name did come up in the desultory two weeks' talk? If such a thing *was* mentioned, the spellbound Drummond certainly would not have failed to scribble it down.

54 "on the first Friday of" — Kay, *Jonson*, 100, quoting from Coryat's letter of 1616. As attendees, Coryat mentions Jonson and John Donne, among others, as regulars, but not Shakespeare.

CHAPTER FIVE: *TREMOR CORDIS*

As explained above, this chapter deals with facts laid out and treated earlier, so here a minimum of source citation is needed.

56 **The adultery charge against Susanna**: What I see as the utterly devastating effect of this ugly incident on Shakespeare has left no direct evidence of itself in the record, that is, aside from his promptly going to law. The point to be understood, better than it is now, is the way the sensational charge would have swept through town, becoming the central topic at every table, then lingering on in the town's memory to be gossiped about for years (despite Susanna's apparent exoneration in court). The adultery accusation was bad

enough to start with, but what made it infinitely worse of course was the added claim about Susanna having contracted a venereal disease — it isn't at all clear which way that charge was meant to cut, that Susanna caught the infection from Ralph Smith, or gave it to him. When the full story of this bizarre episode is finally unearthed, as surely someday it will be, I think it will prove to have had quite considerable bearing on the poet's final end, in the direction I suggest. Especially will this be true with reference to the Lane-Greene link, though digging it out from the scattered and obscure documents will not be easy.

56   **Concern over Judith**: In Shakespeare biography, for no adequate reason, Judith is almost always portrayed as suffering her father's disfavor. Not marrying until she'd passed thirty, being unable to write (Susanna could), and getting mixed up with Quiney constitute the whole of the evidence, hardly sufficient. It's entirely possible that Judith was *more* in favor than her sister, may in fact have been the smarter and more attractive of the two, and received as much or more of her father's respect and affection. Susanna gets the nod over Judith from biographers only because Shakespeare put his estate into her hands (but perhaps largely because of her level-headed husband), and because she was remembered with a fortunate epitaph ("Witty above her sex," etc.).

Poor Judith's grave has never been located, though the assumption is that she was buried in the cemetery attached to Holy Trinity, the headstone now missing or never erected. When she died in 1661, aged 78, no immediate family survived her, in Stratford or elsewhere, so it can't be said who determined her burial site. One quite interesting possibility, even likelihood, is that she may not have died at home in Stratford. She may, in the late 1650s, have left Stratford permanently and gone up to London to join her erring and absent husband and died there. Or it may have been elsewhere in Warwickshire. Her grandniece, Lady Barnard (Susanna's daughter Elizabeth), was then living a life of comparative luxury at Abingdon, and may have helped her, may have taken charge of her burial.

56–58 **The enclosure threat and agreement**: It is obvious that Shakespeare *could*, like, some other wealthy Stratfordians, have declared himself against enclosure, taking his chances on a big loss while siding with the less fortunate. That he didn't, that he quickly moved to protect his own interests, is a fact that has made many of his modern admirers uncomfortable. All sorts of special pleading has been indulged in to set up a defense. Better simply to admit that, while admirable in so many ways, in this matter, faced with a dire threat to his dream of founding a dynasty through a possible loss of finances, he took the low road.

My suggestion that Shakespeare himself helped to suborn (is that too strong a word?) Greene, acting on behalf of the Combes and Replingham, rests on no direct evidence, only what may be called a matrix of facts and appearances so indicating. That it all finally led Shakespeare, also keenly aware of the link with John Lane, to despise Greene, I think hardly needs argument.

57   **Thomas Greene's role**: Some observers are more easily indulgent about Greene's actions, preferring to exonerate him from any sort of double-dealing in the enclosure fight — not on the evidence but by simple assertion. The surviving documents, however, show that his active work for the Council slacked off after his name was added to the Replingham agreement, halting altogether in early 1615. Chambers, one of the first to study the subject closely, concluded that Greene "was still acting for the Corporation in the matter during March 1615 but thereafter seems to have dropped out, although he continued to note events in his diary up to the beginning of 1617" (*Facts and Problems*, 152; see also Fripp, *Artist*, 811–12; Lee, *A Life*, 476–78; Eccles, *Warwickshire*, 137–38). It was on January 9, 1615, or soon after, that Greene was added to the Replingham agreement. The mere fact of his being simultaneously a party to two opposing agreements — calling for contradictory action and loyalty — I would think is sufficient to condemn him. Within a month of Shakespeare's death he had sold his Stratford house and his interest in the tithes and had moved with his family to Bristol. He died in London about 1640.

58–59 **Revision of the will**: It won't hurt, I think, to make doubly clear my view of the various revisions. Some time *before* January 1616 a will had already been executed by Shakespeare. The revision of January 1616 was done to accommodate Judith's married status. The revision of mid-March 1616 was in response to the two-pronged Quiney trouble (the license and Wheeler affairs). The final change (described in chapters Two and Six) in early April 1616 was done to reflect Shakespeare's gratitude to the friends whose behind-the-scenes maneuvering got Quiney's Bawdy Court sentence reduced.

61   **Shakespeare family deaths**: See the genealogies in Lee, *A Life*, 514–15; Brown, *Shakespeare*, 339; Wilson, *Evidence*, 453–55. For Elizabeth Hall's illness see her father's notes of the case in Hall, *Observations*, 31–34 (case no. XXXVI).

61   "Thus she was delivred" — Hall, *Observations*, xxxvi, pp. 31–34 in the Joseph facsimile. This description of Hall's treatment of his daughter is the longest

in his book, nearly three pages where most are less than a page. The number of "medicines" of all types applied to her is rather amazing. With everything else, she was also afflicted for a time with "an ophthalmia," for which her father prescribed eye-drops of "Ophthalmick Water," not further described. Hall's noting in about 1630 that his daughter recovered "and was well for many years" seems to say that she eventually fell sick again. It is a fact that though married twice, the first time at age eighteen, for a total of forty-four years, she bore no children. With her ended the poet's direct line.

63   **Shakespeare's interference in the Bawdy Court sentence**: The evidence for this, while circumstantial, is in my view strong almost to a certainty. The court sentence was reduced, without explanation. Shakespeare about that time made changes in his will to show affection or gratitude to two close friends, men of influence in Stratford. There is no obvious or surface reason for this belated attention to his two friends, though one is needed. The timing of the additions makes a link with the reduction of the court sentence not only possible, but a good deal more than probable.

66–68 **The Greene-Shakespeare altercation**: That there did take place between the two at New Place a very heated encounter, whether physical or not, I assert as established by the evidence laid out earlier. That it resulted in Shakespeare's suffering an apoplectic seizure I believe is also certain, or nearly so, and that the frightening condition brought on a fear of immediate death or incapacity, making him want to execute his will without delay. I feel sure, in addition, that there must have been a fiery display of resentment and frustration on the part of the enraged poet toward Greene, and that a physical struggle erupted between the two, if a brief one. That moderate conclusion, and the progress of the fight as I describe it — surely begun with Shakespeare exploding in anger — I believe has been fully earned, in any case as a hypothesis, by all that's presented in the pages preceding.

CHAPTER SIX: SERGEANT DEATH

69–70 **Dr. Hall's care of Shakespeare**: Nothing directly places Hall at the poet's sickbed as physician. However, as do most observers, I believe he was there. If not Dr. Hall, who? Further, there does exist one tantalizing mention of the ailing man in Hall's records, one long overlooked. In a letter of May 1790 the great Shakespeare scholar Edmond Malone wrote with frustrating brevity: "I find from Dr. Hall's pocket-book, which was once in my possession, that a Mr. Nason was Shakespeare's apothecary" (quoted without comment in the 1848 Halliwell biography [285]). In Stratford then there were several Na-sons, one a barber-surgeon. Hall's noting who supplied the Shakespeares with medicine must have some significance.

70   "also Hypochondriack" — Hall, *Observations*, 23 (case XXIX).

70   "oppressed with Melancholy" — Hall, *Observations*, 26 (case XXXI).

70   "prepared pearl, prepared" — Hall, *Observations*, 29 (case XXXIII).

70   "Peacock dung, dried" — Hall, *Observations*, 38 (case XLII).

70   "He appears a dedicated" — Joseph, *Son-in-Law*, 47.

70   "He practiced Physik" — Joseph, *Son-in-Law*, 107.

71–72 **Visit to New Place by Sadler**: Necessary, considering the dates involved, and his and Reynolds' efforts at getting the Bawdy Court to relax or rescind its punishment of Quiney. I think the good news of the reduced sentence would have been brought promptly and in person to the sick father-in-law, worried as he was, and that his old friend Sadler would have been the one to do it.

72   **Visit to New Place by friends**: Why wouldn't some of the poet's friends and colleagues from London have come the hundred miles to visit and encourage him during the month of his illness? Heminges and Burbage at least, I conclude, made the journey precisely to urge publication of a collected edition of the plays (why weren't the poems included? Jonson's pioneering *Works* of 1616 did carry many of his poems. Probably it was thought that with thirty-six plays in the Shakespeare volume — as against nine in Jonson's — the book was already too large).

A tradition that surfaced in 1864 supports — if so late a claim can support anything — the suggestion of visitors from London at the poet's sickbed. It held that "he caught his death when leaving his bed when ill because some of his old fellows had called on him," the callers identified as "playfellows" (*Quarterly Review*, April 1864, as quoted in Schoenbaum, *Lives*, 78). If there is anything at all to such a belated report it is certainly not in the suggested cause of death but in the mention of visitors.

74   "incomparably the most"—Blayney, *First Folio*, 1. That, of course, is the judgment of a literary man! Others might suggest other works as most "important," starting, let us say, with Darwin's *The Origin of Species*.

74   "only to keep the memory"—Dedication to the First Folio.

74   "the Author himself had lived"—Introduction to the First Folio. This statement, to my mind, shows unmistakably that Heminges and probably Condell, and perhaps Burbage, had talked with Shakespeare about a collected edition of his plays, and that the poet had at least tentatively agreed.

74   **Fair copy of the will**: There really can be no doubt, I think, that Collins, after these latest changes, intended to make a more finished, more professional copy of the very rough, much-altered document as signed on March 25th. Probably in the ensuing four or five days a fair copy *was* made, the poet's death preventing its signing.

74   **Neglect of Shakespeare by the Council**: This development I offer as fact, but admittedly the evidence is wholly circumstantial, though strongly so. The secret Replingham agreement having, as I show, become known to the Council, it resulted in the shunning of the ailing poet by the town board, all its members thoroughly disappointed and resentful of the influential citizen—suspecting at the same time that it was he who had subverted their formerly trustworthy clerk, Thomas Greene. I conclude that it was Shakespeare's sudden, shocked realization that this doleful result had actually happened, that his family's reputation had received a stain of dishonor, which delivered the final blow to his already desponding heart. Francis Collins being the one who told him about the board's feelings is my own conclusion, quite reasonable, I feel.

75   **Fox and Gibbs**: Members of the Stratford Council, see Fripp, *Stratford*, 11, 53.

76–77 **Possible specific cause of death**: Interestingly, though there is no direct or obvious link to Shakespeare personally, the mention in *A Winter's Tale* by Leontes that "I have tremor cordis on me," explained as "My heart dances, but not for joy; not joy," suggests a possibly relevant speculation. Dancing is not a usual description of heart failure, but it does neatly describe a "fibrillating" heart, the condition known today as atrial fibrillation. In it the heartbeat becomes erratic, interfering with the blood flow and producing a state described in the medical literature as "fluttering." Spontaneous remission can and often does occur, but if the fibrillation long continues a fatal stroke may result. *A Winter's Tale* was written in or about 1611, just before or just after its author retired permanently to Stratford. Atrial fibrillation of a congenital sort may be the true underlying cause of his fatal stroke five years later, acted on by the mental and emotional strains detailed in the text.

CHAPTER SEVEN: FORBEARE TO DIGG

82   **Removal of Susanna**: Lee, *A Life*, 512. This information Lee attributes to an 1871 book, *The Home of Shakespeare*, by Samuel Neil, copies of which have so far eluded my search.

82   **Location of Hall's grave**: His lying beyond Nashe, though he died twelve years before him, I think indicates that the Nashe grave in 1635 as already taken. That in 1647 it was emptied to accommodate Nashe seems likely: if it had stood empty till then there seems no reason why Dr. Hall would not have been laid in it, rather than in the grave beyond.

82   "The scandal of such" — Lee, *A Life*, 486.

82   **Repairs to the gravestone**: Ingleby, *Bones*, 31. This operation may provide an explanation for the curious fact that the gravestone does not bear Shakespeare's name: there is no name at all on the stone, only the four-line warning verse. The present stone may be a replacement, the original perhaps having been cracked or otherwise damaged by the settling of the ground. Perhaps the engraver in 1690 accidentally overlooked the name. On the church wall to the left of the grave hangs the famous monument to the poet, an ornate bust-portrait, and this may later have been deemed sufficient identification or reference. This wall monument, however, provides a little puzzle of its own, since the lengthy inscription declares that the poet lies "within this monument." It is not clear that the reference is to the chancel grave beneath it, and in any case a grave is not a monument. It was a London firm that made the wall-monument, but who wrote the inscription is not known:

> Stay, passenger, why goest thou by so fast?
> Read, if thou canst, whom envious death hath plast
> Within this monument, Shakespeare with whome
> Quick Nature dide; whose name doth deck ys tombe
> Far more than cost; sith all yt he hath writt
> Leaves living art but page to serve his wit.

Whoever wrote the lines — one of the poet's London theater colleagues, it may be — it was apparently expected that they would be affixed to an actual, above-ground monument standing directly over the body. The original plan may have been for a costly and conspicuous tomb somewhere inside the church, and when this proved impracticable the chancel grave was used.

82 **The grave undisturbed**: The desire, or urge, to open Shakespeare's grave in hopes of finding personal items or papers buried with him has periodically popped up among Shakespeareans and others. The latest attempt came in 1962 — anticipating the poet's 400th birthday two years later — when a London Shakespeare society made an official appeal to the Stratford authorities. As stated in the *London Times*, the purpose was "to ascertain once and for all for the benefit of scholars all over the world, whether this tomb contains any manuscripts or contemporary historical evidence bearing on the life and times of the Bard." The request, fortunately, was denied, and never to date has such a wish come close to being granted (fortunately because in this writer's view there is a point at which mere literary curiosity comes second to the superior demand of ordinary life to let the dead sleep in peace).

ADDED NOTE

Two more recent books on Shakespeare, by Stanley Wells (2002) and L. Duncan-Jones (2001), treat the events and incidents of his final year, though without concluding to a pattern of cause and effect. Both reached me after my own studies had been completed.

Duncan-Jones's comments and conclusions (*Ungentle Shakespeare*, 255–79) are both baseless and curiously quirky. Without the least evidence she postulates that Shakespeare died of syphilis, and hated his wife so much he forbade her being buried in the same grave with him (an idea echoed by Greenblatt, also lacking evidence). She does spot the possible significance of early death in the Shakespeare family but lets it go at that.

Wells offers a more measured handling of the relevant incidents, though not linking them with the poet's death. In the matter of Richard Quiney's church punishment for getting the Wheeler girl pregnant he thinks, as I do, that Shakespeare may have intervened to have the punishment lessened. In the enclosure affair he agrees that Shakespeare, rather than siding with the town poor, "succeeded in sitting on the fence, safeguarding his own interests while not offending his rich friends." He also inclines toward my own finding that Shakespeare spent more time at home in Stratford during his stage career than has been thought — "Our first great literary commuter," he calls him.

Greenblatt also treats some of the final events but to no particular effect. The cold self-interest the poet displayed in the enclosure affair he dismisses with a shrug: "Perhaps, as some have said, he believed in modernizing agriculture, and thought that in the long run everyone would prosper; more likely he simply didn't care." He also treats Shakespeare's will and Quiney's troubles with the Bawdy Court but reaches no conclusion.

Selected Bibliography

Listed are those published works cited in the notes, or which have afforded background information or general stimulus. Place of publication unless otherwise stated is New York or London.

Ackroyd, Peter. *Shakespeare: The Biography*. 2005.

Adams, Joseph Quincy. *A Life of William Shakespeare*. 1923.

Arlidge, Anthony. *Shakespeare and the Prince of Love: The Feast of Misrule in the Middle Temple*. 2000.

Barton, N. "Dr. John Hall." *Journal of Medical Biography* 8 (2000): 17–24.

Bearman, Robert. *Shakespeare in the Stratford Records*. Stratford. 1994.

Bentley, Gerald Eades. *Shakespeare: A Biographical Handbook*. New Haven, CT, 1994.

Blayney, P. W. M. *The First Folio of Shakespeare*. Washington, DC, 1991.

Bond, Edward. *Bingo* (A play). Woodstock, IL. 1974.

Brassington, William Salt. *Shakespeare's Homeland: Sketches of Stratford-upon-Avon, the Forest of Arden and the Avon Valley*. 1903.

Brinkworth, E. R. C. *Shakespeare and the Bawdy Court of Stratford*. 1972.

Brown, Ivor. *Shakespeare*. 1949.

Burgess, Anthony. *Shakespeare*. 1970.

Chambers, Edmund Kerchever. *William Shakespeare: A Study of Facts and Problem*. 2 volumes. 1930; repr. 1966.

Chute, Marchette. *Shakespeare of London*. 1949; repr. 1996.

Duncan-Jones, Katherine. *Ungentle Shakespeare: Scenes from His Life*. 2001.

Eccles, Mark. *Shakespeare in Warwickshire*. Madison, WI, 1961.

Elton, Charles Isaac. *William Shakespeare: His Family and Friends*. 1904.

Fripp, Edgar Innes. *Shakespeare's Stratford*. 1928.

———. *Shakespeare: Man and Artist*. 2 volumes. 1938.

Gray, Arthur. *Shakespeare's Son-in-Law John Hall*. 1939.

Gray, Joseph William. *Shakespeare's Marriage, His Departure from Stratford and other Incidents in His Life . . . .* 1905.

Green, Adwin Wigfall. "Shakespeare's Will." *Georgetown Law Journal* 20 (1932): 273–92.

Greenblatt, Stephen. *Will in the World: How Shakespeare Became Shakespeare.* 2004.

Greenwood, Sir George G. *Shakespeare's Handwriting.* 1920.

———. *The Shakespeare Signatures and "Sir Thomas More."* 1924.

Greer, Germaine. *Shakespeare's Wife.* 2007.

Hall, John. *Observations on English Bodies.* 1657. (reprinted in Joseph, *Shakespeare's Son-in-Law,* see below.)

Halliday, F. E. *A Shakespeare Companion.* 1964, repr. 1968.

Halliwell-Phillipps, James Orchard. *The Life of William Shakespeare. Including Many Particulars Respecting the Poet and His Family Never before Published.* 1848.

———. *Outlines of the Life of Shakespeare.* 1886.

Hamilton, Charles. *In Search of Shakespeare: A Study of the Poet's Life and Handwriting.* 1986.

Hanley, Hugh A. "Shakespeare's Family in the Stratford Records." *Times Literary Supplement.* May 21, 1964.

Holden, Anthony. *William Shakespeare: His Life and Work.* 1999.

Honan, Park. *Shakespeare: A Life.* 1998.

Honigman, E. A. J. "The Second Best Bed." *New York Review of Books.* (38.18) Nov. 7, 1991.

Hotson, Leslie. *I, William Shakespeare, Do Appoint Thomas Russell, Esquire.* 1937.

Ingleby, C. M. *Shakespeare's Bones. The Proposal to Disinter Them, Considered in Relation to Their Possible Bearing on His Portraiture: Illustrated by Instances of Visits of the Living to the Dead.* 1883, repr. 2010.

———. *William Shakespeare and the Enclosure of Common Fields at Welcombe: Being a Fragment of the Private Diary of Thomas Greene, Town Clerk of Stratford-upon-Avon, 1614–1617.* 1885.

Joseph, Harriet Bloomfield. *Shakespeare's Son-in-Law: John Hall, Man and Physician. With a facsimile of the 2d ed. of Hall's "Select observations on English bodies."* Hamden, CT, 1964.

Kay, Dennis. *Shakespeare: His Life, Work, and Era.* 1992.

Kay, W. David. *Ben Jonson: A Literary Life.* 1995.

Lane, Joan. *John Hall and His Patients: The Medical Practice of Shakespeare's Son-in-law.* Stratford-upon-Avon, 1996.

Lawless, Donald S. "On Shakespeare's Death, Funeral, and Burial." *Notes & Queries.* 27 (1980): 176–77.

Lee, Sidney. *A Life of William Shakespeare.* 1916.

Leftwich, Ralph W. "The Evidence of Disease in William Shakespeare's Handwriting." *Proceedings of the Royal Society of Medicine, Section of the History of Medicine* 12 (1919):28–42.

Levi, Peter. *The Life and Times of William Shakespeare.* 1989.

Lewis, Benjamin R. *The Shakespeare Documents.* Stanford, CA, 1940–1941; repr. Westport, CT, 1969.

Lindley, Walter. "Dr. John Hall, William Shakespeare's Son-in-Law." *The Medical Record.* May 20, 1916.

MacDonald, M. "A New Discovery about Shakespeare's Estate in Old Stratford." *Shakespeare Quarterly* 45 (Spring 1994):87–89.

Marcham, Frank. *William Shakespeare and His Daughter Susanna.* 1931.

Masson, David. *Drummond of Hawthornden: The Story of His Life and Writings.* 1873.

Miles, Rosalind. *Ben Jonson, His Life and Work.* 1986.

Milward, Peter. "Shakespeare and Catholicism." *Shakespeare Yearbook* (Spring 1990):133–40.

———. *Shakespeare's Religious Background.* 1973.

Mitchell, C. Martin. *The Shakespeare Circle, a Life of Dr. John Hall, Shakespeare's Son-in-law, with Glimpses of Their Intimate Friends and Relations.* Birmingham, 1947.

Mitchell, Reg. *Tho. Quiney—Gent: Shakespeare's Son-in-law.* London, 2003.

Newdigate, Bernard H. *Michael Drayton and His Circle.* Oxford, 1961.

Norman, Charles. *So Worthy A Friend: William Shakespeare.* 1947.

O'Connor, Gary. *William Shakespeare: A Popular Life.* 2000.

Patterson, R. F., ed. *Ben Jonson's Conversations with William Drummond of Hawthornden.* London, 1923; repr. New York, 1974.

Phillips, Graham, and Martin Keatman. *The Shakespeare Conspiracy.* 1994.

Price, Diana. "Reconsidering Shakespeare's Monument." *Review of English Studies* 48 (May 1997):168–82.

Quennell, Peter. *Shakespeare, the Poet and His Background.* 1963.

Riggs, David. *Ben Jonson: A Life.* Cambridge, MA, 1989.

Rogers, Joyce. *The Second Best Bed: William Shakespeare's Will in a New Light.* Westport, CT, 1993.

Rowse, A. L. *William Shakespeare: A Biography.* 1963.

Schoenbaum, Samuel. *Shakespeare's Lives.* 1970, repr. 1991.

———. *William Shakespeare and Others.* Washington, 1985.

Severn, Charles. *The Diary of Rev. John Ward Vicar of Stratford-upon-Avon, Extending from 1648 to 1679. From the Original MSS. Preserved in the Library of the Medical Society of London.* 1839.

Simpson, Robert Ritchie. *Shakespeare and Medicine.* Edinburgh, 1959.

Speaight, Robert. *Shakespeare: The Man and His Achievement.* 1977.

Stalker, Archibald. "Is Shakespeare's Will a Forgery?" *Quarterly Review* 274 (1940): 48–57.

Stopes, C. C. *Shakespeare's Environment.* 1914.

Tannenbaum, Samuel A. *A New Study of Shakespeare's Will.* Baltimore, 1926.

———. *Problems in Shakespeare's Penmanship, Including a Study of the Poet's Will.* 1927.

Thompson, Edward Maunde. *Shakespeare's Handwriting.* Oxford, 1916.

———. *Shakespeare's England*, London, 1928.

Trussler, Simon. *Will's Will: The Last Wishes of William Shakespeare.* Kew, Richmond, UK, 2007.

Webster, Margaret. *Shakespeare without Tears.* Cleveland, OH, 1955.

Wells, Stanley. *Shakespeare: For All Time.* 2003.

Williamson, Hugh Ross. *The Day Shakespeare Died.* 1962. (A speculation concerning Shakespeare's possible Catholicism, suggesting that a priest attended his deathbed.)

Weiss, René. *Shakespeare Unbound: Decoding a Hidden Life.* 2007.

Wilson, Ian. *William Shakespeare: The Evidence: Unlocking the Mysteries of the Man and His Work.* 1994.